Neue Perspektiven der Medienästhetik

Series Editor

Ivo Ritzer, Bayreuth, Germany

Die Reihe „Neue Perspektiven der Medienästhetik" versteht sich als Brückenschlag zwischen Ansätzen von Medientheorie und ästhetischer Theorie. Damit sollen ästhetische Qualitäten weder als determinierende Eigenschaften einer technologisch-apparativen Medialität noch als Effekt dieses medialen Apriori begriffen sein. Stattdessen werden sowohl die Relevanz des Technologisch-Apparativen als auch die im Rahmen der apriorischen Konstellation sich entfaltende Potentialität an ästhetischen Verfahren ernst genommen. Die Frage nach medienästhetischen Qualitäten bedeutet demnach, die einem Medium zur Verfügung stehenden ästhetischen Optionen zu spezifizieren, um ihrer Rolle bei der Konstitution des jeweiligen medialen Ausdrucks nachzuspüren. Dabei projektiert die Reihe insbesondere, entweder bislang vernachlässigte Medienphänomene oder bekannte Phänomene aus einer bislang vernachlässigten Perspektive zu betrachten.

More information about this series at http://www.palgrave.com/gp/series/13443

Christoph Ernst · Jens Schröter
Editors

(Re-)Imagining New Media

Techno-Imaginaries around 2000 and the case of "Piazza virtuale" (1992)

Editors
Christoph Ernst
Rheinische
Friedrich-Wihelms-Universität
Bonn, Germany

Jens Schröter
Rheinische
Friedrich-Wihelms-Universität
Bonn, Germany

ISSN 2524-3209 ISSN 2524-3217 (electronic)
Neue Perspektiven der Medienästhetik
ISBN 978-3-658-32898-6 ISBN 978-3-658-32899-3 (eBook)
https://doi.org/10.1007/978-3-658-32899-3

© The Editor(s) (if applicable) and The Author(s), under exclusive license to Springer Fachmedien Wiesbaden GmbH, part of Springer Nature 2021
This work is subject to copyright. All rights are solely and exclusively licensed by the Publisher, whether the whole or part of the material is concerned, specifically the rights of translation, reprinting, reuse of illustrations, recitation, broadcasting, reproduction on microfilms or in any other physical way, and transmission or information storage and retrieval, electronic adaptation, computer software, or by similar or dissimilar methodology now known or hereafter developed.
The use of general descriptive names, registered names, trademarks, service marks, etc. in this publication does not imply, even in the absence of a specific statement, that such names are exempt from the relevant protective laws and regulations and therefore free for general use.
The publisher, the authors and the editors are safe to assume that the advice and information in this book are believed to be true and accurate at the date of publication. Neither the publisher nor the authors or the editors give a warranty, expressed or implied, with respect to the material contained herein or for any errors or omissions that may have been made. The publisher remains neutral with regard to jurisdictional claims in published maps and institutional affiliations.

Responsible Editor: Barbara Emig-Roller
This Springer VS imprint is published by the registered company Springer Fachmedien Wiesbaden GmbH part of Springer Nature.
The registered company address is: Abraham-Lincoln-Str. 46, 65189 Wiesbaden, Germany

Inhaltsverzeichnis

Introduction 1
Christoph Ernst and Jens Schröter

Past and Present Metaphors of Interaction and Virtuality 7
Sally Wyatt

The Promise of the Promise—The Dynamic Medium Group in Oakland, California 15
Götz Bachmann

Imagination *via* Demonstration—Performing Interactive Television and the Case of *Piazza virtuale* (1992) 31
Christoph Ernst and Jens Schröter

Televisionen/Television/Televisuality/Televirtuality. Imaginary of TV in the 1980s and 1990s 47
Oliver Fahle

Deconstructing Cyberpunk Worlds—Technodystopian Imaginaries in the Storyworld of Gibson's Neuromancer 63
Wenzel Mehnert

Piazza Virtuale—The Public Sphere and Its Expansion Beyond the Physical 89
Hannah Glauner

**Reimagining *Piazza virtuale*—A Conversation
with Van Gogh-TV** 111
Christoph Ernst, Jens Schröter, Karel Dudesek,
Benjamin Heidersberger, Salvatore Vanasco, and Mike Hentz

Autorenverzeichnis

Götz Bachmann Universität Bremen/Leuphana Universität Lüneburg, Lüneburg, Germany

Karel Dudesek Wien, Austria

Christoph Ernst Rheinische-Friedrich-Wilhelms-Universität, Bonn, Germany

Oliver Fahle Institut für Medienwissenschaft, Ruhr-Universität Bochum, Bochum, Germany

Hannah Glauner Humboldt-Universität zu Berlin, Berlin, Germany

Benjamin Heidersberger Berlin, Germany

Mike Hentz Berlin, Germany

Wenzel Mehnert Universität der Künste Berlin, Berlin, Germany

Jens Schröter Rheinische Friedrich-Wihelms-Universität, Bonn, Germany

Salvatore Vanasco Berlin, Germany

Sally Wyatt Maastricht University, Amsterdam, Netherlands

Introduction

Christoph Ernst and Jens Schröter

> **Abstract**
>
> The Introduction contextualizes the main argument of the book within the context of media theoretical discussions at the end of the twentieth century and provides an overview over the contributions of the book.

The era at the end of the twentieth century was characterized by the simultaneity between traditional mass media such as newspapers, radio and television and the development of digital media and their integration in all areas of daily life. In the 1980s and 1990s, discussions on the possibilities of using the "Computer as medium" (Andersen et al. 1993; Bolz et al. 1994) became a central topic of social imagination. Postmodern debates about "Digital images" (Mitchell 1992), "Hypertext" (Bolter 1991), "Cybertext" (Aarseth 1997) and "Multimedia" (Nielsen 1995), and "Interactivity" (Jensen and Toscan 1999) are emblematic for the emergence of new media practices in those years. Keywords like "Virtual Reality" (Rheingold 1991), "Simulation" (Baudrillard 1994), "Rhizome" (Deleuze and Guattari 1987) or "Cyberspace" (Barlow 1996) marked a transformation of the public sphere. In connection with political events like the end of the Cold War and the Gulf War in 1991 new ways of thinking about the effects on media on society emerged (Schröter 2004). This thinking was decisively influenced by the projected impact of computer-based media technologies on society ("Future

---

C. Ernst (✉) · J. Schröter
Rheinische-Friedrich-Wilhelms-Universität, Bonn, Germany
E-Mail: cernst@uni-bonn.de

J. Schröter
E-Mail: schroeter@uni-bonn.de

shock", Toffler and Toffler 1971) and eventually found its expression in terms such as "Network Society" (Castells 1996).

From today's perspective, these older debates are both anachronistic and relevant at the same time. They not only provide an insight into the expectations and hopes of this epoch, but also show to what extent the imagination of new media is itself a driving factor in media development (Natale and Balbi 2014). New media are never simply 'new' (Hansen 2010), but the fact that they are considered to be 'new' articulates a promise of the future that inevitably brings the imagination into play (Ernst and Schröter 2020). Media technologies, like all technologies, are embedded in what Sheila Jasanoff and Sang-Hyun Kim (2015) have termed "sociotechnical imaginaries." Against this backdrop 're-imagining' a past future means more than just remembering a forgotten utopian or dystopian future. "Re-imagining" is an act in which a bygone future that once surrounded a 'new' medium is rediscovered, even re-enacted, with regard to those aspects that—despite the fact that the medium is no longer 'new' and perhaps even forgotten—still make the fundamental principles of that medium relevant in contemporary discourse.

Of particular importance in this context are imaginaries of media in popular culture and media art, which were a primary context for negotiating the effects of digital technologies on society. Not well known—yet historically very important—with regard to videoconferencing and interactivity is e.g. the project *Piazza virtuale* by the media artist group *Van Gogh TV*, which will be given special consideration as a case study in this book. *Piazza virtuale* was the attempt to develop an interactive television, thus reshaping relation between television and the public sphere. Realized on *documenta IX* (1992) in Kassel, it was the largest experiment ever undertaken to implement interactive television on a global scale. Unique in the history of television, the project is an excellent example to discuss and analyze the question how artistic and performative aspects of media practices (in this case practices of 'doing television') are intertwined not only with various ideas about the future of the public sphere but also with opposing concepts and agencies of media use, the factual realities of available technologies and different facets of (media-)theoretical reflections on the possibilities of 'old' and 'new' media. On the basis of examples like this, the book asks how the social imaginaries that developed around "new" media developed and how this development can be theoretically grasped.

(1) In the first text Sally Wyatt discusses the eminent role of metaphors for the imagination of new media. Metaphors of 'new' media from the 1980s and 1990s still resonate today. With regard to Van Gogh TVs *Piazza virtuale* she analyzes the basic metaphor of the 'virtual' implied in the project title. In particular, the text

discusses the imagination of an alternative public sphere as one of the prototypical tropes of early visions of a new networked medium. (2) Relying on ethnographical field-studies on the "Dynamic Medium Group" in the San Francisco Bay Area, the second text by Götz Bachmann analyzes the relation between 'new' media and the future by focusing on its character as a "promise". As Bachmann shows, promises can be regarded as "analytical tools" to situate imaginaries of future new media in specific social relations, thus opening up an important alternative to traditional ways of analyzing especially the relation between new media and the future. (3) The aspect of socially situating imaginaries is also a key aspect of the third text by Christoph Ernst and Jens Schröter. Expanding on the 'performative' side of Jasanoff's and Kim's definition of "sociotechnical imaginaries" the authors argue that media art can be discussed by using research on technology demonstrations (public experiments etc.). The text discusses key concepts in this field (e.g. Wally Smiths "Theatre of Use") and applies these perspectives on *Piazza virtuale*. (4) In the fourth contribution Oliver Fahle zooms in on the relation between television and the imaginary. As Fahle illustrates, television changes substantially the 1980s, eventually leading to a medium, which is, as Fahle points out, in early 1990s regarded as the state of the art of media technology. Combining the notion of the imaginary with an intriguing reading of the German term "Televisionen", he uses the term "Televirtuality" to analyze this new status of television. His text demonstrates the relevance of notions of 'virtuality' in electronic media which are not related to what is today commonly referred to in rather crude ways as computer-based 'digital media'. (5) This leads back to the time, when the alliance between computers and virtuality was forged, the early 1980s, and in particular the concept of "Cyberspace", which is addressed in the fifth text by Wenzel Mehnert. Mehnert revisits the seminal texts of William Gibson. Reading the concept of "cyberspace" through the lenses of theoretical concepts like Jasanoff's and Kim's "sociotechnical imaginaries", he demonstrates how these "technodeterministic" narratives encapsulated in the cyberpunk-movement of the 1980s can be re-imagined (and criticized) with regard to our contemporary understanding of Science Fiction. (6) In her discussion of Van Gogh-Tvs *Piazza virtuale* Hannah Glauner goes back to the topic of the public sphere as the main focal point of the metaphor of *Piazza virtuale*. Explicating the historical depth of the metaphor, her analysis focusses not so much on the aspect of virtuality realized by technical media, but on the architectural metaphor of the 'Piazza'. Analyzing how this spatial metaphor is realized in an interactive medium, she demonstrates how the metaphor helped the users of the system to adapt to the new modalities of an early form of 'on-line' interaction. (7) The book closes with an interview with the media artist group Van Gogh-TV themselves. Remembering their main projects *Piazza virtuale* (1992) and *Service area a.i.* (1994), the artists give a vivid impression of how they conceived their ideas and, more importantly, were able to realize them given the conditions of their era. The interview gives rare insights in the practices of 'doing media art' and thus represents an important document for further analysis of the legacy of Van Gogh-TVs work and the practices of 'imagining' in media art in general.

This book presents results of the research project "Van Gogh-TV. Multimedia-Documentation and Analysis of their Legacy" (Prof. Anja Stöffler, Prof. Dr. Jens Schröter) funded by the German Research Foundation (DFG). It contains contributions from the workshop "(Re-)Imagining New Media Cultures in Art and Popular Culture at the End of the 20th Century," 11/12th October 2019 at Rheinische Friedrich-Wilhelms-University Bonn. The editors would like to thank Dana Adscheid, Leila Brehme, Anna Gößl, Vimbai Hühner and Karoline Kozlowski and for their great help in editing the manuscript.

References

Aarseth, Espen. 1997. *Cybertext: Perspectives on ergodic literature*. Baltimore, MD: Johns Hopkins University Press.
Andersen, Peter B., B. Holmqvist, and J.F. Jensen, eds. 1993. *The computer as medium*. Cambridge: Cambridge University Press.
Barlow, John Perry. 1996. A declaration of the independence of cyberspace. Electronic Frontier Foundation. https://www.eff.org/cyberspace-independence. Accessed 10 July 2020.
Baudrillard, Jean. 1994. *Simulacra and simulation*. Ann Arbor: The University of Michigan.
Bolter, J. David. 1991. *Writing space. The computer, hypertext, and the history of writing*. Hillsdale: Erlbaum.
Bolz, Norbert, F.A. Kittler, and G.C. Tholen, eds. 1994. *Computer als Medium*. München: Fink.
Castells, Manuel. 1996. *The rise of the networked society*. Malden: Blackwell.
Deleuze, G., and F. Guattari. 1987. Introduction: Rhizome. In *A thousand plateaus: Capitalism and schizophrenia Part II*, 3–25. Minneapolis: University of Minneapolis Press.
Ernst, Christoph, and J. Schröter. 2020. *Zukünftige Medien. Eine Einführung*. Wiesbaden: Springer VS.
Hansen, Mark B. N. 2010. New media. In *Critical terms for media studies*, ed. W.J.T. Mitchell and M.B.N. Hansen, 172–185. Chicago: University of Chicago Press.
Jasanoff, Sheila, and S.-H. Kim, eds. 2015. *Dreamscapes of modernity. Sociotechnical imaginaries and the fabrication of power*. Chicago: University of Chicago Press.
Jensen, Jens F., and C. Toscan, eds. 1999. *Interactive television. TV of the future or the future of TV*. Aalborg: Aalborg University Press.
Mitchell, William J. T. 1992. *The reconfigured eye. Visual truth in the post-photographic era*. Cambridge: The MIT Press.

Natale, S., and G. Balbi. 2014. Media and the imaginary in history. *Media History*. https://doi.org/10.1080/13688804.2014.898904.

Nielsen, Jakob. 1995. *Multimedia and hypertext: The internet and beyond*. San Francisco: Kaufmann.

Rheingold, Howard. 1991. *Virtual reality. The revolutionary technology of computer-generated artificial worlds – A how it promises to transform society*. New York: Simon & Schuster.

Schröter, Jens. 2004. *Das Netz und die virtuelle Realität. Zur Selbstprogrammierung der Gesellschaft durch die universelle Maschine*. Bielefeld: transcript.

Toffler, Alvin, and H. Toffler. 1971. *Future shock*. New York: Bantam Books.

Past and Present Metaphors of Interaction and Virtuality

Sally Wyatt

Abstract

Since its very early days, metaphors have been used by more and less powerful social actors to try to convey what the internet is and what it can or should be used for in the present and in the future. In the mid-1990s, when the internet went public and the World Wide Web became available, many different metaphors were in use as people tried to make sense of the possibilities of this powerful new medium, capable of instantly transmitting data and information around the world. This chapter briefly reviews the varied metaphorical past of media and digital technologies, and then explores the metaphorical connotations and richness of *Piazza virtuale*, the interactive television project created by Van Gogh TV, a collective of artists and engineers.

Keywords

Metaphor • Internet • Television • Interactivity • Virtual

1 *Only Connect*, EM Forster

Whenever new media forms have been introduced, from the printing press onwards, they have been accompanied by recurring dreams, nightmares, hopes and fears. To make new media comprehensible and acceptable to new audiences and publics, references are made to the similarities with and differences from past

S. Wyatt (✉)
Maastricht University, Amsterdam, Netherlands
E-Mail: sally.wyatt@maastrichtuniversity.nl

© The Author(s), under exclusive license to Springer Fachmedien Wiesbaden GmbH, part of Springer Nature 2021
C. Ernst and J. Schröter (eds.), *(Re-)Imagining New Media*, Neue Perspektiven der Medienästhetik, https://doi.org/10.1007/978-3-658-32899-3_2

media (Bolter and Grusin 2000). Furthermore, metaphors are often deployed to help people make sense of the new and emerging possibilities. In this chapter, I look at the metaphors about the internet and related technologies that were beginning to circulate when *Piazza virtuale* was on air[1] in the early 1990s.

Elsewhere (Wyatt 2004, 2021) I have examined the ways in which social actors deploy metaphors to convey what the internet and other digitally based technologies are and how they could be used in the future. Following George Lakoff and Mark Johnson (1980), I argued that metaphors can be used to serve particular political, technical or economic interests, and that those in power are often able to impose their metaphors and ideas about the future in an effort to realize those ideas in some material form. In this short chapter, I focus on the early 1990s, when *Piazza virtuale* was being developed and used. The next section provides some context, focusing on the convergence of computing and telecommunications and on other experiments in community television from earlier decades. I then discuss metaphors of interaction, both individual human–machine interactions and the more collective engagements stimulated by *Piazza virtuale* and other such experiments. The final section focuses on the metaphors of *piazza* and virtual, highlighting what could have been. In Science and Technology Studies (STS), this idea of possibility and potentiality is central, and captured by the phrase "that [technologies] might have been otherwise" (Bijker and Law 1992, p. 3). Similar ideas are also present in media archaeology (Elsasesser 2004) and philosophy of technology (Feenberg 1999).

2 Convergence and Community

Before the internet and World Wide Web moved beyond the scientific community to commerce, entertainment, politics, and everyday sociality in the mid-1990s, there had been many other attempts to connect computers, using different standards and interfaces. At the time, there was much talk of the "convergence" of computers and telecommunication, enabling the same data, in digital form, to be accessed by many devices in different locations. Convergence was not only a technical accomplishment but also an economic and policy restructuring of two hitherto distinct industries. The predominantly private corporations producing computers were organized and regulated very differently from the largely public telecommunications sector (at least in Europe). This convergence also transformed

---

[1] "On air" is itself a metaphor, that has now lost its novelty and is part of everyday language, in English at least. Note that metaphors are very language-specific.

information and communication activities, blurring the boundaries between personal communication via post and telephone, long-standing newspaper, magazine and book publishing, and the mass media of radio and television that had taken off earlier in the twentieth century. Already in the 1980s, what were variously called "value added network services" or "new interactive services" (Thomas and Miles 1989) had been emerging. Many services taken for granted by 2020 were beginning to be available, often in experimental form, and often prefaced by "tele-" in the case of shopping and banking. Online databases, electronic mail and bulletin boards, and travel reservation systems were also being developed in the latter decades of the twentieth century.

There were precedents for these growing (inter)actions at a (great) distance (Latour 1992). Alexander Graham Bell imagined the telephone would be used to allow people in rural areas to listen to concerts performed live in major concert halls. At the end of the nineteenth century, in parts of Europe concerts and talk programmes were transmitted to households via sophisticated cable systems. There were many experiments from the 1950s through the 1980s in using community video to involve local communities not only in the consumption of programming but also in its production. Rod Allen and Nod Miller (2000) provide many examples of this, focusing on the United States. The combination of geography, privately owned broadcasting, and constitutional commitments to free speech made the United States a fertile environment for experiments in community-based video. They illustrate how at the time many considered that community video could offer "broadcast town meetings" (Allen and Miller 2000, p. 51), as a form of local, participatory democracy, resonant of Habermas' (1989) notion of the public sphere.

In the same volume, Herbert Pimlott (2000) examines the Canadian situation, which shares the geographical features of the US, namely a very large area with people living in remote areas in which broadcasting technologies of the time did not always function. However, Canada had a different political economy of broadcasting. The Canadian Broadcasting Corporation (CBC) is a national, public broadcasting agency modeled on the British Broadcasting Corporation (BBC). Canada also had (and still has) a National Film Board (NFB). The NFB was committed to social documentary, and developed a portable kit enabling local communities to produce their own videos, on topics relevant to their concerns. Pimlott (2000, p. 99) describes it as "an attempt to meet public demands for access to the public sphere through the new media." Pimlott goes on to note how this was another instance of the "conflict between the private sphere (economic interests) and/ the public sphere (political interests)" (2000, p. 99–100). During the same period, media ownership in Canada and the US (and in many other western countries) became increasingly concentrated in a smaller number of private corporations, something which is happening again with digital media (van Dijck et al. 2018). In the next section, I return to the Habermasian public sphere, and the more general archetypes and metaphors circulating in the 1990s about the internet.

3 Archetypes and Metaphors

In an anthology of writings called *Internet Dreams*, Mark Stefik organizes the metaphors that emerged around the internet into four fundamental archetypes: keeper of knowledge, communicator, trader, and adventurer. He argues that these "have long guided our technological visions" (1996, p. xxii), and as the preceding section illustrates, they were also to be seen in the experiments around community television.

Metaphors of interaction for personal computing abound, to the point where some have become taken for granted, such as "desktop" for the visual interface of computer screens, and "windows" for one of the major operating systems. "Personal assistants" are re-entering the lexicon, especially with voice-activated services. But they have a longer history, such as "Clippit," the animated paper clip that used to pop up on people's computer screens, usually unasked, to offer advice on how to use Microsoft Word. The standard visual icons for "phone" and "mail" recall a time of rotary dial telephones and paper envelopes, but nonetheless remain in use in digital environments. These linguistic and visual metaphors are largely about individual human–machine interactions.

What interested the artists who designed *Piazza Virtuale* were the possibilities for collective interaction. Both *piazza* and *virtuale* have important connotations, to which I return in the next section, but they also resonate with other metaphors reflecting the "communicator" archetype identified by Stefik. For example, community video experiments were often described using metaphors of town hall, village square, agora, and forum. The same metaphors appeared repeatedly in the early days of the internet. Such metaphors were deployed to stress the deliberative and communicative spaces offered by online discussion. These were in marked contrast to the "trader" archetype reflected in online shopping malls or the "keeper of knowledge" captured by metaphorical invocations of libraries and world brains.

The metaphors of open and public deliberation referred implicitly or explicitly to the concept of "public sphere" developed by Jürgen Habermas (1989). The metaphors mentioned in the preceding paragraph all invoke past ideals of public deliberation in which everyone can speak, and be heard by fellow citizens and by those in power. The early days of the internet were characterized by the hope that the technical possibilities were finally in place to realize a fully functioning public sphere that gave voice not only to elites but also to publics and counter-publics. All other technologies of communication, including television and video, have been characterized by similar hopes.

Since those early days of internet optimism, the situation has changed. The production, control and ownership of key aspects of internet infrastructure and provision in western democracies[2] have become concentrated in the hands of a small number of American corporations. All act to secure their global dominance through acquiring small companies, imposing technical standards throughout their supply chains, and lobbying governments to implement regulation favourable to their interests.

In the next section, we return to those heady days when real-time interactions at a distance offered artists, technicians, journalists, political activists, and many others with the possibilities to explore and experiment with new forms of engaging publics and audiences.

4   Piazza Virtuale

Piazza virtuale was created by Van Gogh TV, a collective of artists and technicians from Austria and Germany who had first started working together in the mid-1980s. *Piazza virtuale* was an interactive television project that could be received throughout Europe for 100 days during *documenta IX* in Kassel, Germany in 1992. Those wishing to participate could connect using telephone, fax or modem to the live broadcast via videophones and cameras that had been permanently installed in Kassel and other European cities. The project reversed the dominant television relationship of one broadcaster and many receivers into an interactive medium (*documenta archiv* no date). In many ways, it was similar to the community video experiments mentioned earlier.

Van Gogh TV, the artistic collective, and *Piazza virtuale*, the *documenta IX* project, are discussed more extensively elsewhere in this book. In this chapter, I focus on the name. The project precedes the widespread diffusion of the internet that started in mid-1990s, but, as already mentioned, the technical possibilities

---

[2]The situation in China and other parts of the world is very different, but beyond the scope of this chapter.

for communicating across distance involving multiple participants had long been available.

Piazza simply means "open town square" in English. As such, it is in line with all of the other spatial metaphors that were used to describe online communication, borrowed from other languages (such as *agora*), or from the past (such as "village square"). All invoked times and places of meaningful interaction and debate, and simultaneously celebrated romanticized notions of the past.

Virtuale is more complicated, even though it is a Latin word that has been taken up in most European languages. But it is not at all straightforward in its meaning when applied to new, digital media. In the 1990s, it was often adopted as a prefix, to denote anything in online environments, such as virtual communities or virtual organizations, or to denote simulated spaces, as in virtual reality. But sometimes it was highly normative, and contrasted with "real," so that friends and communities in the physical realm of everyday life were considered more authentic and meaningful than anything that might be taking place in "cyberspace".

There were many other additions, prefix or suffix (though in English usually as prefix or adjective), in circulation throughout the 1990s. These include cyber-, tele-, electronic, online, distance, and computer-mediated. As with virtual, all of these promise something new, and a future which will be faster and better. In practice, there are always tensions between new and old, between change and tradition. This is particularly the case with the introduction of new technologies, which are always introduced into social contexts which have established histories, and ways of doing things. If and how new technologies are adopted at all, whether they succeed or fail, or change in use are always open to the particular contexts of incorporation and domestication.

These tensions point to a longer philosophical line of reasoning in which "virtuality" is a mode of reality bound up with potentials and emergence (Massumi 1998). The connection to the future remains, but virtual is also generative, creative and open. In this way *Piazza virtuale* is not simply an artistic experiment in online broadcasting, it also carries a potential for change, in this case change in the one-to-many form of broadcasting that had become dominant in the second half of the twentieth century. By enabling people throughout Europe to engage with each other in real-time, it opened up new possibilities that became technically easier as the internet expanded its influence from big science to everyday life.

There are many more recent examples of artists opening up new possibilities, challenging corporate and state domination of digital technologies. For example, Patricia de Vries and Willem Schinkel (2019) analyze artworks, such as masks and other forms of camouflage, that aim to challenge the surveillance capacities of facial recognition technologies. They draw on Søren Kierkegaard's conception of anxiety and the desire for possibility to understand the algorithmic anxieties materialized by such technologies. De Vries and Schinkel see masks as offering a new form of subjectivity, "that call[s] for an imagination that is not wedded to human-machine dualisms" (de Vries and Schinkel 2019, p. 11). They find a way to use Kierkegaard, often cited as the father of existentialism, to offer hope in a world in which digital technologies are increasingly deployed to increase surveillance both by the state and by privately owned technology corporations.

In this chapter, I have re-visited community-based and artistic experiments in using media that were new at the time to draw attention to the ways in which metaphorical language and practical imagination can open up new possibilities and challenge dominant modes of use and interaction. *Piazza virtuale* offers a fascinating example, combining both artistic and community elements. Moreover, the use of *piazza* resonates strongly with the Habermasian notion of public sphere and its metaphorical equivalents of communicator that have long accompanied new media forms. Most importantly, almost thirty years later, *Piazza virtuale* still offers hope by providing an example of a materialized imagination in which alternative forms of interaction and engagement are possible.

Acknowledgements I am very grateful to Christoph Ernst and Jens Schröter for their invitation to join the workshop "(Re-)Imagining New Media in Art & Popular Culture at the End of the 20th Century" held in Bonn in October 2019. I am indebted to them, the other participants, and the members of the Van Gogh TV media artists' group for their comments and contributions. It was a very inspiring event.

References

Allen, R., and N. Miller. 2000. Panaceas and promises of democratic participation: Reactions to new channels from the wireless to the world wide web. In *Technology and in/equality: Questioning the information society*, ed. S. Wyatt, F. Henwood, N. Miller, and P. Senker, 46–60. London: Routledge.

Bijker, W., and J. Law. 1992. General introduction. In *Shaping technology/building society. Studies in sociotechnical change*, ed. W. Bijker and J. Law, 1–14. Cambridge: The MIT Press.

Bolter, Jay David, and R. Grusin. 2000. *Remediation. Understanding new media.* Cambridge: The MIT Press.

De Vries, P., and W. Schinkel. 2019. Algorithmic anxiety: Masks and camouflage in artistic imaginaries of facial recognition algorithms. *Big Data & Society.* https://doi.org/10.1177/2053951719851532.

documenta archiv. no date. Processing and research of the work of the artists' collective 'Van Gogh TV'. https://www.documenta-archiv.de/en/archiv/projekte/1237/processing-and-research-of-the-work-of-the-artists-collective-van-gogh-tv. Accessed 20 Feb. 2020.

Elsaesser, T. 2004. The new film history as media archaeology. *CiNéMAS: Revue d'Études Cinématographiques* 14 (2–3): 75–117.

Feenberg, Andrew. 1999. *Questioning technology*. London: Routledge.

Habermas, Jürgen. 1989. *The structural transformation of the public sphere*. Translated by Thomas Burger. Cambridge: The MIT Press.

Lakoff, George, and M. Johnson. 1980. *Metaphors we live by*. Chicago: University of Chicago Press.

Latour, Bruno. 1992. Where are the missing masses? The sociology of a few mundane artefacts. In *Shaping technology/building society: Studies in sociotechnical change*, ed. W. Bijker and J. Law, 225–258. Cambridge: The MIT Press.

Massumi, Brian. 1998. Sensing the virtual, building the insensible. In *Hypersurface Architecture*, Ed. Stephen Perella. *Architectural Design* 68 (5–6): 16–24.

Stefik, Mark. 1996. Introduction. In *Internet dreams. Archetypes, myths, and metaphors*, ed. Mark Stefik, 1–5. Cambridge: The MIT Press.

Pimlott, Herbert. 2000. Limited Horizons (inc.): Access, democracy and technology in community television in Canada. In *Technology and in/equality: Questioning the information society*, ed. S. Wyatt, F. Henwood, N. Miller, and P. Senker, 86–108. London: Routledge.

Thomas, Graham, and I. Miles. 1989. *Telematics in transition. The development of new interactive services in the United Kingdom*. Harlow: Longman.

van Dijck, José, T. Poell, and M. de Waal. 2018. *The platform society. Public values in a connective world*. Oxford: Oxford University Press.

Wyatt, Sally. 2004. Danger! Metaphors at work in economics, geophysiology and the internet. *Science, Technology & Human Values* 29 (2): 242–261.

Wyatt, Sally. 2021. Metaphors in critical internet and digital media studies. *New Media & Society* 23 (2): 406–416.

The Promise of the Promise—The Dynamic Medium Group in Oakland, California

Götz Bachmann

Abstract

When researching the often-exuberant promises that accompany new technologies and new forms of computational media, we navigate the seas between the Scylla of pure description (or worse: naïve celebration), and the Charybdis of all too easy deconstruction or critiques of others' ideology. For a successful voyage, we need theoretical tools and approaches that allow fine-grained analysis of prospective practices. In my analysis of fieldwork among a very specific group of engineers in the San Francisco Bay Area—a research collective working towards a radically new idea of computational media—I employ the notion of the promise, as it was developed in the sociology of expectations, as well as in some newer contributions in Science and Technology Studies. The results are terminological suggestions, some of which are newly developed by drawing on the differences in meaning of three possible translations of the term promise in the German language: "Versprechen", "Versprechung" and "Verheißung". The paper concludes with a plea to extend the analysis of the promise to the ways that we as ethnographers, authors and readers are dragged into in the social constellations of promises. After all, we are part of these constellations, as promisees, as potential witnesses, and as fellow-promisers. As much as the analysis of promises implies us to be "reluctant to judge too quickly" (Fortun 2005, p. 170), a reflective approach also allows for more than only detached analysis.

G. Bachmann (✉)
Universität Bremen/Leuphana Universität Lüneburg, Lüneburg, Germany

Keywords

Medium • Promise • Expectation • Dynamicland

1   The Dynamic Medium Group

Since 2015 I have been conducting ethnographic fieldwork in the "Dynamic Medium Group", a small non-profit research collective based in the San Francisco Bay Area that started its work in 2013, and aims to build a fundamentally new medium. The head of the Dynamic Medium Group, Bret Victor, is an engineer in his early 40s, and one of the most daring and controversial figures, when it comes to conceptualizing, what a computational medium is and could be. Before founding the Dynamic Medium Group, Bret Victor worked for a few years at the notoriously secretive Apple Cooperation. Before and after this period at Apple, he had produced a series of widely noted public prototypes, talks and essays, exploring information design, human–computer interfaces, the autonomy of engineering, the history of computing, and the computer as a medium for the sciences, among other topics. The group is heavily influenced by these ideas, as well as by those of engineering and design legends Doug Engelbart and Alan Kay. Alan Kay is furthermore also the group's patron, and helps generate its funding. Crucial in this is the legendary status of Kay: In the late 1960s and 1970s, Kay wrote a series of papers about an emerging dynamic medium (e.g. Goldberg and Kay 1977), based on heavy doses of Marshall McLuhan and developmental psychology on the one hand, and engineering and design work on the other, which included early iterations of graphical user interfaces, object oriented programming languages and operating systems, and prototypes for computers designed to be used everywhere by everyone—all of which are from today's perspective important conceptual contributions to the emergence of many of the traits of digital media that we now take for granted.

The Dynamic Medium Group places itself in the tradition of research of the "Augmentation Research Centre", led by Engelbart in the 1960s, and the "Learning Research Group" at Xerox PARC, led by Kay in the 1970s, yet it questions their outcomes. To the group, those technologies that are often considered as being influenced by the past research of these groups—screen-based private computers, such as workstations, smart phones, smart watches or tablets, running graphical user interfaces, and connected in large networks—are, in the view of the Dynamic Medium Group, a social and cultural disaster. They broke their promises: of making us more creative, helping us think better, or of connecting us. Indeed, in the view of the group, digital media, as they have become, had the opposite effects: we are lonely in front of a myriad of screens, our thinking got corrupted by screen-focused GUIs (bad), or writing-based programming languages (worse), our democratic institutions are undermined in the horrendously designed world wide web, malevolent mega-corporations reign, and cultural, economic, political and environmental threats are unfolding without us finding ways to think about them, let alone act upon them. The group thus aims for a radical re-set, and for this they need, so their argument, conditions like their precursors in the 1960s and 1970s: The ability to work as engineers and designers on a long term project of a fundamentally new medium, with open outcome, no deadlines or deliverables, and the fullest possible absence of commercial or academic pressures or logics. Only this could enable them to develop a better computational medium.

This, of course, is a breathtakingly ambitious and elitist project. In the last five years, the group was, however, able to generate industry funding for 7 researchers, almost all of them educated at US elite institutions such as the MIT, to work under these conditions, first in San Francisco's South of Market District, and then, across the Bay, in Central Oakland. In the first two years since its start in 2013, the group built hundreds of prototypes, which then culminated in one bigger and joint project named "Dynamicland". This mother of all prototypes took most of the following two years to build. Dynamicland is a hybrid of space and computer. What we otherwise encounter on a screen—either in a text-based programing environment or in a GUI—is spread out all over the room. "People walk around" in a "real place," where "real objects in physical space" take over the role of "virtual objects on a screen."[1] Dynamicland is thus neither a variation of VR nor AR, but a space filled with things, some of which are computational objects (for those who are familiar with programming paradigms: in Dynamicland, the objects of object-oriented programming have physical properties). Therefore, Dynamicland allows its inhabitants, amongst other traits, to

---

[1] These quotes are taken form a "Zine" that the group collectively wrote in Spring 2017.

program in space (this is also the reason, why Dynamicland is not at all another version of the Internet of Things, but, once more, the opposite). Programming is lucid and fully controlled by humans (distinguishing it from Artificial Intelligence and Machine Learning). And all this includes not only programming further applications in Dynamicland, but also programming Dynamicland itself: The operating system that runs Dynamicland is built in Dynamicland. Or, to be a little more precise: a hybrid between an operating system and a programming environment named "Realtalk", which the group has built to run Dynamicland, is, at least in significant parts, built in the computationally enhanced room that is run by the same system: Realtalk does not only run Dynamicland, but it also runs *in* Dynamicland, indeed, it was to large parts developed in Dynamicland, and can now, at all times, be changed inside of Dynamicland, using its own properties. Dynamicland runs itself.

After two years of building it, the first iteration of Dynamicland works. The overall technical assemblage still needs external support (the group calls this "scaffoldings"), but it is functional, and at its core it is functional autonomously. And its properties are indeed impressive. The group, however, argues that Dynamicland is only a glimpse at something much, much bigger. What's at stake here, according to the group, is not only technology. It is a fundamentally new "dynamic spatial medium" in emergence. This medium would enable us to use the potentials of computational thinking in a "more real" and "human-scale" way. It would allow us to see complex interdependencies, and help us to think, express and communicate "new thoughts", unthinkable before. To demonstrate the scale of the ambition: the group believes that this medium will make new thoughts possible in fields ranging from the analysis of complex systems all the way to mathematics. Such thoughts, whether old or new, would now, due to the simplicity and transparency of this fundamentally new medium, be communicable to everyone, and thus up to debate and scrutiny. Its spatial nature and absence of screens would also enable us to develop new forms of "togetherness" and cure many of the social ills the group perceives as being caused by current, screen-based computational devices. Indeed, this is a form of computing that makes little sense, if only used by an individual: It would thus be a form of computing that has to be run by communities, and not by networked individuals and large corporations.

This might sound like a wish list run out of control, but at least the first glimpses of many of these properties can already be observed and experienced if you visit Dynamicland: It is quite a magical place, and many of its visitors, ranging from some of the tech elites of the Silicon Valley all the way to kids from neighbouring low-class and non-white backgrounds, agree, after having played in and with Dynamicland for a few hours. I am using words like "magical" and "play", because it is hard to put into words, and for sure hard to communicate how it "feels" to anyone, who has not been there. The group takes all this as an encouragement that its overall project has merits: if the dynamic spatial medium would establish itself within the next few decades, it could, if we think small, start a media-induced revolution similar to the one induced by personal computers and the internet, or, if we want to think bigger, the historic shifts induced by printing, or even writing. And if this medium would exist, it would make a substantial contribution to an even larger project: Nothing less than a contribution to preventing that "the world tears itself apart". Such claims are pretty hard to digest, even in Silicon Valley, which is not exactly a stranger to big promises.

2 From Hyperbole to "Versprechung" and "Verheißung"

In the field of Science and Technology Studies, the promise is both a topic of analysis, and an analytical device. It is not surprising that one of the first observations is often the hyperbole of promises in regard to the potential consequences of innovations in the field of technology and media. However, in the more advanced analysis of promises this is usually followed by a second, crucial twist: Just as much as the initiation rite for serious thinking about futures is to negate futurology (in the sense of making actual predictions about the future), the initiation rite to the analysis of promises seems to be that the analyst starts seeing hyperbole as something that needs to be understood, and not lamented. For Sarah Franklin (2001, p. 349, italics by the author), it is "a mistake to think that we can somehow factor out the hype, the media or the work of the imagination to exaggerate either the promises or the risks of new technology. *This is not going to be possible, now or in the future, because it is precisely the importance of imagining a future yet-to-be*". Instead, we should understand the "links between the hype, the product, the market, the science, the Government and the goodwill of the general public" (ibid.).

In the sociology of expectations, as developed by Harro Van Lente, Arie Rip, Kornelia Konrad, Nik Brown and Mike Michael, we can find hints, how to theorize this further: Promises take place and take part in early phases in the "dynamics of expectations", which are often characterised by "escalating arguments for and against". They will thus be often "inflated, and have to be inflated in order to get a hearing" (Brown et al. 2003, p. 3). According to the sociology of expectations, "initial promises are set high in order to attract attention from (financial) sponsors, to stimulate agenda-setting processes (both technical and political) and to build 'protected spaces'" (Geels and Smit 2000, p. 882, drawing on van Lente 1993). Promises thus play different roles at different stages, and they change their character, while doing so: Initial promises tend to be broad, later promises tend to be more concrete. Harro van Lente proposes that some of these processes are cyclic: Once promises come close to their (necessarily partial) realization, they kick off new promises. Furthermore, we are not only looking at one promise, but at a series of "nested" promises: "broader, encompassing promises (…) may help to protect more specific promises" (Brown et al. 2003, p. 4). This nesting can be followed all the way into very broad promises, such as the cultural ideas of scientific and technological progress.

Once you apply this framework to the Dynamic Medium Group work, a plurality of nested promises become immediately visible: the promise that a fundamentally new medium is possible; the promise that Dynamicland gives us a glimpse at such a new medium; the promise that this medium will help to address all sorts of problems; and the promise that addressing such problems is possible at all—to name only some of the most basic promises. But there are also other promises, which are more related to the way of working of the group: The promise that brilliant engineers, if left to their own devices, can create something amazing; as well as the promise of autonomy to the engineers, who work in the group. Furthermore, we can see promises in regards to the history of the work of the medium, such as the promise that the work of the Dynamic Medium Group has a similar potential like the work at Xerox PARC, and that the work at Xerox PARC has left us with unfulfilled promises, which are, a further set of promises, not obsolete, but more relevant than ever, as well as finally realisable now.

If we push all this a little further into the realm of artefacts, we can see even more promises. Not only can we understand the plural function of the demos. The latter are promise-artefacts, which are to be read as a promise, as evidence for the promise, and as promising even more than what it evidences, all at the same time. We can also see how members of the group scan their prototypes for promises—promising features, which point to bigger things than the simple traits of that particular prototype. And we can see how the group understands their overall work process as one driven by the promise of the power of media: By building a first iteration of a digital medium, which the group then uses to build another iteration of the medium, they hope to lift themselves up with their own bootstraps, into a media-induced evolution of their own abilities as researchers and engineers and the media they develop, just as Doug Engelbart has famously promised it to his own research group and his funders more than half a century ago (Engelbart and English 1968). The Dynamic Medium Group promises itself into existence. Its outcomes are then used both as verifications of the feasibility of these promises, and as promise-making entities themselves, led by and leading to even bigger promises about a better digital medium for a better future, if all this ever comes to the fore. To borrow a term, which the members of the research group use to describe their own practice of prototyping: The Dynamic Medium Group is a "scaffold" of promises, where each promise supports the others and the overall daring construction reaches a dizzying height—and this scaffold itself holds the promise that in its midst grows a solid building that will make all of this worthwhile.

This form of radical engineering operates inside of what ANT-inspired scholars have started to call a "promissory assemblage": just as much as the "promissory assemblage" of a city contains "the multiple ontologies of urban assemblages as a promise of the city, as the promised city and urban promises" (Färber 2020, p. 270), here, too, we have a mix of the promise of digital media, of promised digital media, and of specific promises made by engineers as central actors in the field. Yet, in the field of digital media, promises have also worn off significantly: At least in the view of Alan Kay, Bret Victor, and the young researchers of the Dynamic Medium Group (and also in the view of the author), Silicon Valley has long given up on putting its focus on the generation of new ideas, and instead concentrates mostly on scaling up older ideas such as Artificial Intelligence into large infrastructures mostly for the purpose of evermore extraction of value and increase of power. This makes the re-installation of the claim of the ability to engineer radical difference an uphill battle. Part of this battle is waged simply by doing it: "By proposing a plan, or by making a promise, the producers of the plan are constituting themselves through indexical self-reference: a performative act presumes performers, and by performing the act of 'I promise,' they index themselves as such performative persons" (Abram and Weszkalnys 2013, p. 10). But the members of the Dynamic Medium Group have to do more: They have to both revitalize and shift the promissory assemblage of digital media, as much of the old one has lost its credit. This is not without potential tragedy, but it also creates a space of negotiation and critique, a re-opening of the promissory assemblage that enables them and us to question what is, what the future is supposed to be, and what alternatives we have.

Part of the task of the group is thus to recreate the openness of the future of digital media, against a feeling that contemporary futures of the Silicon Valley are closed. In this they build on what Mike Fortun calls in his analysis of the Human Genome Project the "excess of promising" (2005, p. 171). Fortun demonstrated this with a reading of Nietzsche's and Arendt's ideas about the promise. Whereas Hannah Arendt's reading of the idea of the promise in Nietzsche has, according to Fortun, "shrunk" the promise "to the level of a human assertion that establishes 'an island of certainty' in a future marked by radical uncertainty", Fortun insists that "Nietzsche's promise, science's promise, is not an anchoring device", but "the risky affirmation of a recurring, iterative opening." (ibid., p. 175). Indeed, the promise can be both: on the one hand it can catch the future in a semi-contract between the promiser and the promisee. We might call this a "handshake-promise": promiser and promise both know what they are in for, with a future, where they can compare the envisioned with the factual outcomes, and a presence where they both evaluate the likelihood of a positive evaluation in the future. On the other hand, a promise can also be what one might call, drawing on Fortun, an "opening-promise." Usually such an opening is not without direction, but also not yet fully clear. Indeed, promiser and promisee might not be fully on the same board.

What we slowly see is that calling a promise a promise is not enough. We need to work on our terminology for different aspects, different shades and different versions of promises. Some we have already encountered: we have, by now, not only the "promise", but also "the promiser" and "the promisee", both of whom become, what they are, once the promise is made. We have the "promise-as-speech-act", which is, at least if we stay closely with Austin's original analysis, always bound to the speech act of the promiser, and should not be analysed from the perspective of its alter ego, the promisee (Austin 1962). We also have the opposite, the "promissory assemblage", a term that encompasses not only both promisers and promisees, but also artefacts, discourses, ideas, infrastructures … indeed, the whole bag of ANT's "multiple ontologies". We have "promises-as-handshakes", where promises take the role of semi-contracts, and promiser and promisees operate on the same plane, yet, of course, in different roles. And we have "opening-promises", which are always more than what they explicitly entail. The latter, the "opening-promises", produce their own social constellation, and they seem, to me, particularly important, if we want to understand the Dynamic Medium Group. I therefore suggest in the following two further terms, which describe aspects of this particular constellation of the opening-promise.

The first one is the "promise-as-Versprechung". I am switching to a German term, as the German language has a range of different translations on offer for the term "promise". The most common one is "Versprechen", and I think it is reasonable to use this both for the overall class of all promises, and in the context of the "handshake-promise". However, there is also "Versprech*ung*". This, too, means "promise", but it is more often used, when combined with the attributes "vage" ("vague") and "leer" ("empty") or with the verb "glauben schenken" (giving the gift of believing). Without these attributes, a "Versprechung" is not automatically vague or empty, but it still has the connotation of a more open, less explicit, and not fully complete promise. I thus suggest to use "promise-as-Versprechung", when we describe a rather open, not yet fully sharpened promise, made by a promiser, not yet fully accepted by the promisee, yet maybe considered, and, for sure, luring and stirring thoughts, actions or desires in its direction. Think of moments, when someone might entice you to take a job with vague statements of what might be possibly possible, or to invest in technology, or to believe in communism: all are promises-as-Versprechungen, and they have effects, many of whom are productive. But contracts they are not. Indeed, when they are made, the promiser might not even have a clear idea of who the promisees are: She or he might just make an open promise, directed to whoever is hearing this. If a promisee takes this on, she does not make a metaphorical handshake to enter a semi-contractual agreement. She might, however, do something more: she might turn into a semi-believer—one that always has the question in the back of her head, whether the attribute "empty" should not be added. She believes with doubts.

While promise-as-Versprechung starts in a constellation of an opening-promise with what the *promiser does*, a "promise as-Verheißung" starts on the other side, and situates the promise in what the *promisee finds* (which is, of course, also a form of doing something). We can thus, for example, find, or "see", a promise-as-Verheißung in a landscape. Other examples are some of the moments, when the engineers in the Dynamic Group analyse artefacts, which they themselves have built. Sometimes, though not always, they do this to *find* promises-as-Verheißungen: they look for that, what is promised to them in the artefacts of their own making. Such situations occur often after the members of the group were "carried away" in the process of producing the prototype. A second version occurs, when the engineers in the group engage in "riffing". Similar to Jazz-musicians, they explore the promises-as-Verheißungen of one prototype by immediately building a second prototype that is loosely inspired by the first one. Such forms of riffing occur in the Dynamic Group quite often, and they are encouraged and cherished. They are especially productive if done collectively, and prototypes of different engineers are explored by the prototypes of others. A further version is Dynamicland itself: It is built to enable a myriad of further apps, many of whom can only be envisioned, once Dynamicland exists. Building applications in Dynamicland is thus a form of exploring its promise-as-Verheißung. All this does not mean that all material practices, or even all prototyping, is a search for promises-as-Verheißung. A demo, for example, is the opposite: it is a representation of a promise-as-Versprechung in the form of an artefact: Whoever builds it, takes the role of a promiser. A promise-as-Verheißungen, on the other hand, starts with the promisee as the main agent. Yes, the promisee concentrates on "the other side", the potential promiser, which can be a human or artefact or anything else, but it is the promisee, who turns the promiser into a promiser. Once more we have a slightly paradoxical constellation: On the one hand, the promisee can find his or her promiser everywhere. The agent is the promisee, not the promiser. On the other hand, this works only if the promisee opens up to the potential promiser, taking its potential seriously and letting its promise-as-Verheißung take over.

These two additional terms can both describe moments that stand on their own: There are promises-as-Versprechung, which are not matched by promises-as-Verheißung, and the other way round. However, often they do connect, and if they do, they form the full social constellation of an opening-promise. Sometimes, promises-as-Versprechung and-as-Verheißung combine in a perfect match. But more often they connect in more or less productive misunderstandings, forming indirect connections, which share at least some traits with the boundary objects that Susan Leigh Star was so interested in. Different actors with different interests, and, sometimes, different ontologies, can thus connect in loose, yet sometimes powerful constellations that stir thought, desires and action in the directions of some futures, and not others. If they do so, they form a full opening-promise.

3 We, the Promisees, and We, the Fellow-Promisers

In the last step of my argument I want to make some remarks on our own relations to our subject matter. If I say "our", I mean here not only myself, the ethnographer and author of this text, but also you, the reader, as well as the wider academic field of critical enquiries into media and technology in the Social Sciences and Humanities and in the wider public. Surprisingly, such a reflexive approach is still largely uncharted territory in the literature on promises. A notable exception is the already mentioned anthropologist Mike Fortun, who argues that an "ethics of promising and friendship" demands "for us in science studies (…) the continual opening of ourselves, in a series of close encounters of our own invention". Fortun gives us an account of the promise, in which he himself as an analyst is not written out, but placed in its midst. His celebratory idea of the excess of promising (an idea that led me into the suggestion that I developed at the end of the last sub-chapter) entails a plea to "construct new assemblages in which experimental practitioners from both the sciences and science studies can 'muddle through' together toward mutual understanding and even practical ends – uneasily, to be sure, but abetted by the same combination of laughter, dedication, forbearance born of sustained proximity, and mutual critique that characterizes the best friendships in the personal domain." (ibid., p. 170). Building on this approach, I want to sketch out how reflexivity has become important in my own work.

The ideas of the Dynamic Medium Group are promises-as-Versprechungen. As such, they are also directed to *us*, among others. They try to lure us in. We are addressed. We are in it. Promises-as-Versprechungen ask us to be not only promisees, but believers. Such gestures, especially when they come from a research group situated in the Silicon Valley, are bound to generate an anti-reaction. No text embodies this anti-reaction in such a clear form as the "Californian Ideology" by Richard Barbrook and Andy Cameron (1995). In this text, two European Scholars polemicized in the mid 1990s brilliantly against the Californian merger of techno-solutionism with cultural and economic forms of libertarianism—so brilliantly, that the suspicion of "Californian ideology" is almost automatically evoked, whenever European scholars of a critical, left-wing bend (and I would count myself as one of these) take a look at anything in the Silicon Valley. However, the text is also a reaction that is rooted in a deep disappointment of European scholars, written at a moment, when their own lofty dreams in the promises of a new networked culture started to turn sour. When we react with the label "Californian ideology", we stay inside the constellation of a past and "broken" promise, and transfer it to contemporary phenomena. Often, this makes sense. But for the Dynamic Medium Group, it does not. The group's goals are anti-corporate and anti-libertarian, and their attempts to reinstate technology and media as a historical forces are, at least, more subtle, than conventional forms of technosolutionism. The group does not think that they can simply "solve problems". Rather, they try to make something like: crucial contributions to instigating a process which might result in the creation of a condition of possibility, which, in their view, would be necessary to then, in conjunction with other necessary conditions of possibility, possibly enable us to address problems. In short: It is a much looser construction. All this still involves building prototypes for new media and new technology, but calling this solutionism would mean that all engineering is the latter. Which would not make sense. To sum up: The work of the Dynamic Medium Group is not without influences of its Californian environment (yes, they, too, love Buckidome and Steward Brand). But their work is much more a distinctly Californian reaction *against* the Californian Ideology. This, in turns, does not mean that the Dynamic Medium Group is immune to contributing to another wave of Californian techno-economic hegemony, in the larger scheme of things, and against their intention. But that is, for now, an open question, and not one, that we can decide already now, simply by recurring to past disappointments.

There is a second reason, why promises-as-Versprechungen in our fields can cause strong (anti-)reactions in us. We are not only potential promisees and believers, we are also fellow-promisers. Our own practices as critical scholars are full of promises, too. They entail handshake-promises ("I am going to write this paper") just as much as bigger promises-as-Versprechungen, ranging from "this paper makes a contribution to our knowledge" all the way to "there are alternatives to the current forms of capitalism". Many of these promises-as-Versprechungen are rather open, not fully explicated, and maybe even a little bit embarrassing. In relation to a field like the Dynamic Medium Group, we see our own promising practices mirrored in the promising practices of them. Mirroring, especially if it feels like mirroring in a distorted mirror, can lead, once more, to aggression—and in this case a very unproductive one. But exactly this mirroring can also be made productive. One example to do so would be to explore the mirroring effects of media theory of the McLuhanite and Kittlerian kind with the approaches of the Dynamic Medium Group. In this paper, I go down a different route and explore the equally striking parallels of the Dynamic Media Group's narratives about futures, and those of left radical thinking. To make this a bit more precise, I use Franco Berardi's idea about "Futurability" (2017) for this analysis.

Franco Berardi is a proponent of what you might call the Italian school of Deleuzian Marxism. He describes the contemporary state of futures in an ontological framework of "possibility", "potency" and "power". While insisting that constant emergence in the presence always produces myriad, but not infinite, amount of possibilities, including the many possibilities that do not actualize, he diagnoses for the last decades a dramatic decline of "potency". With "potency", Berardi describes the "condition that enables transformation – according to the will of a subject". Without it, we are bound to give in to "power", which is, for him, the reign of a "gestalt" that selects and forms possibilities in ways that iterate the same. Under conditions of Impotency, "invention" is "merely a technical improvement of the tools, not any change in the goals of the process itself" (ibid., p. 225). And exactly this has become the case: For Berardi, the reign of capitalism has become total, as mindlessly networked and tracked individuals allow no more potency. My point is: The Dynamic Medium Group shares this view of the future, at least in principle. The similarities are not only superficial. The Dynamic Medium group operates on a thin layer of hope on top of a very dark worldview, occupied by narratives that are structured strikingly similar. And the resulting affects are similar, too: The affective states of despair, depression and impotence which Berardi (and, in his footsteps, Fisher 2014) describes, are never far, also not on a personal level. This does not mean that Berardi, Deleuze, or Marx have influenced the group. But the affects are similar, as are the worldviews.

The similarities become even more striking, if we look how Berardi, on the one hand, and the Dynamic Medium Group, on the other hand, analyze the more recent history: Just as Berardi, the engineers in the Dynamic Medium Group identify the mid 1960s to mid 1970s as the moment, where their respective heroes (for Berardi this is the workers movement, for the Dynamic Medium Group the bold conceptual work on the new digital medium) got something only *half* right, and thus helped to bring about something fundamentally wrong. For Berardi this was the focus on labor in the labor movement. For him, this killed the labor movement, and opened up the gates to an even more vicious iteration of capitalism. For the Dynamic Medium group it was the focus on screens and personal computers. It opened up the gates to an evil caricature of the dynamic medium that gelled horribly well with capitalism. In both cases, their analysis propels them to go back to this time. And both do this to somehow repair this historic mistake by starting anew: For Berardi, it is the idea to re-install the solidarity he experienced in Northern Italy in the 1960s and 1970s, but under conditions of today and the contemporary stage of the "general intellect", now playing out between engineers, artists and designers, who might revitalize morphogenesis, a.k.a. future. For the Dynamic Medium Group it is the work on the medium under similar circumstances as in the 1970s, yet with the knowledge of what went wrong since then, and with the contemporary possibilities of technology at hand. Both know that this promise is out of time: desperate, maybe impossible. But for them, it is the last hope left.

It is thus indeed tempting, to insert the work and the ideas of the Dynamic Medium Group in such a Marxist-Deleuzian framework, and read the work of the Dynamic Medium Group as an attempt towards what Berardi calls "morphogenesis" by engineers and artist. The theorist Berardi imagines that a new opening of futures would start with some kind of "platform" for the joint work and the flow of ideas between artists and engineers. Without any real idea, how such a platform could work, Berardi remains at this point in his analysis stuck in artschool-marxism. One could thus argue that the Dynamic Medium Groups has the better answer to Berardi's quest. However, for now I would not go so far. For one, we should not forget the differences (simply put: the Dynamic Medium Group does not consist of a band of Deleuzian-Marxist in disguise), and simply overlaying the promises would mean to level out the group's more complicated other traits. As much as non-positivist, critical, ethnographic research often includes the search for promises-as-Verheißungen to us—moments in our fields that give us reason for hope, or tell us about meaningful alternatives to our contemporary rather miserable state of affairs—such promises-as-Verheißungen cannot simply be another promise, not only a promise-as-Versprechung made in the field.

But even without such a simple solution, this analysis was not futile. Firstly, a reflexive analysis like the one that I just started to sketch out helps us to not get caught in the affects of mirroring, or of being addressed as promisees. Secondly, we can learn more about our and their promises, if we compare them in both the way they work and what they promise: the respective promises take shape, we can see their strengths and weaknesses, and we can learn from each other. And thirdly, such analysis might not provide us with a ready-made theoretical framework, but it opens up new opportunities of a different kind: We can decide, whether we can and want to co-construct joint constellations of opening-promises. This is less an analytical than a political decision. In respect to the analysis that I have just made, and in my own case, my doubts in regard to Deleuzian-Marxist politics let me hesitate to do so. My worries about other constellations of opening-promises, such as the constellations between the Dynamic Media Group and its industry funders (and their ideas about potential future uses of this technology) add to my doubts. But my political experience also tells me that messy mixes with partners, with whom I agree only partially, are often the only way to gain some political traction. In short: in regard to this political question, I have not found my final answer. But I am still searching. And so can others. I recommend it to do so. The ideas of the Dynamic Medium Group are worth it. And the need to re-create better ideas about how we can re-envision radically different and possible futures, and create coalitions and constellations that work towards them, is more urgent than ever.

4 The Promise of Analysing the Promise

The promise is not only a topic. It is an analytical device, too. As such, it allows us to understand imaginaries about futures, while they are *made*, and when they *play* out. Contrary to other approaches of analyzing imaginaries, which allow the former, too, the promise as an analytical device places imaginaries in a social *constellation* with different roles, practices, and relations between promises and promisees. (Social) rationality is thus here not only a general demand but built into the analytical device. In this paper I have argued that this already substantive analytical power increases even more, if we further refine our terminology. The groundwork for this can be found in the sociology of expectations and in the anthropological corners of Science and Technology Studies. But there is scope for more! Promise-theory has a largely yet unexplored hunting ground for inspiration in the rich philosophical traditions of thinking about the promise—not only the often-used Austin, but also in Nietzsche, Hume, Derrida, or in analytical philosophy (the latter was a loose inspiration in this text, see Scheinman 2011). With terms such as promiser and promisee, promise-as-speech-act, nested promises and promissory assemblages, promise-as-handshake and opening-promise, as well as, introduced in this paper, promise-as-Versprechung and promise-as-Verheißung, we can refine our analysis.

Especially the latter forms of promises have one additional, important quality: They are well-equipped to develop an analysis of promises that includes our own stances, ideas, and relations in the overall picture. Once we do so, we will often not find stable answers, but more a field of questions and political decisions: We can use similarities and differences between their and our promises to make mirroring effects productive—as such we can understand more about our own and the field's forms of promising. We can use this to learn from each other, asking ourselves whether the weaknesses that we see in *their* promises might also be the ones in ours, and vice versa. We can also ask ourselves, whether we want to and can broker constellations of joint opening-promises. Such an analysis of promises can make our own involvement more understood, more enlightened, more politically conscious, and more productive. This, to me, is the biggest promise of analyzing the promise.

References

Abram, S., and G. Weszkalnys. 2013. Elusive promises: Planning in the contemporary world. An introduction. In *Elusive promises*, ed. S. Abram and G. Weszkalnys, 1–33. Oxford: Berghahn.

Austin, John L. 1962. *How to do things with words*. Oxford: Clarendon Press.

Barbrook, Richard, and Andy Cameron. 1995. The californian ideology. https://www.metamute.org/editorial/articles/californian-ideology. Accessed 15 April 2021.

Beradi, Franco. 2017. *Futurability: The age of impotence and the horizon of possibility*. New York: Verso Press.

Brown, Nik, A. Rip, and H. Van Lente. 2003. *Expectations in & about science and technology*. A background paper for the 'expectations' workshop of 13–14 June 2003.

Engelbart, Douglas, and Willaim English. 1968. A research center for augmenting human intellect. *Proceedings of the AFIPS 1968 Fall Joint Computing Conference 9–11* 1 (33): 395–410.

Färber, Alexa. 2020. How does ANT help us to rethink the city and its promises? In *The Routledge companion to actor-network theory*, ed. A. Blok, I. Farias, and C. Roberts, 264–272. London: Routledge.

Fisher, Mark. 2014. *Ghosts of my life: Writings on depression, hauntology and lost future*. Winchester: zero books.

Fortun, Mike. 2005. For an ethics of promising, or: A few kind words about James Watson. *New Genetics and Society* 24 (2): 157–173.
Franklin, Sarah. 2001. Culturing biology: Cell lines for the second millennium. *Health* 5 (3): 335–354.
Geels, F., and W. Smit. 2000. The social function of promises and expectations in technological developments. *Futures* 32: 867–885.
Kay, A., and A. Goldberg. 1977. Personal dynamic media. *Computer* 10 (3): 31–41.
Sheinman, Hanoch, ed. 2011. *Promises and agreements: Philosophical essays*. Oxford: Oxford University Press.
Van Lente, Harro. 1993. *Promising technology: The dynamics of expectations in technological developments*. Utrecht: Eburon.

Imagination *via* Demonstration—Performing Interactive Television and the Case of *Piazza virtuale* (1992)

Christoph Ernst and Jens Schröter

Abstract

Following the assumption that imagination consists of social practices of 'imagining,' the text sketches the theoretical premises for such an idea by claiming that an STS-based approach towards the performativity of technology demonstrations can give valuable insights for the discussion of media art. In the third part we will discuss the problem how temporality, imagination and performativity are intertwined in technology demonstrations. The text concludes with an argument regarding the relation between media art and the problem of the 'future' of new media.

Keywords

Imagination • Demonstration • Technology • Piazza virtuale

1 Introduction

Imagination is not only an individual cognitive faculty of the subject but associated with a set of practices share by a collective. Imagination depends on social factors. Practices of imagining are e.g. characterized by the aesthetics of staging and public demonstration. From the perspective of the arts, this 'performative'

C. Ernst (✉) · J. Schröter
Rheinische Friedrich-Wilhelms-Universität, Bonn, Germany
E-Mail: cernst@uni-bonn.de

J. Schröter
E-Mail: schroeter@uni-bonn.de

aspect of imagination is by no means a new insight. Traditionally the connection between art and imagination has been explained by its fictious character (Walton 1990). However, neither are all forms of art fictional, nor is the social reality beyond art free of different forms of staging—quite the contrary (Goffman 1973). A broad set of forms of demonstration exists in social reality in which imagination is addressed in a way that is not 'aesthetic.' These practices of imagining serve other purposes than aesthetic experience, most notably the attempt to persuade an audience of the viability of an imagined future. In technology for example, demonstrations are used to convey an exemplary idea of what is 'possible,' since the early modern times particularly with regard to the invention of new technologies such as new media.

In this essay we want to draw attention to a very specific aspect of the theory of "sociotechnical imaginaries" (Jasanoff and Kim 2015)—the interconnection between imagination and the different forms of demonstrations of new media technologies. Following research in Sociology and Science and Technology-Studies (STS) we consider technology-demonstrations of new media as consisting of a spectrum of public presentations–from presentations to an audience of experts within rather enclosed contexts to product presentations by major companies (Rosental 2013, p. 344). Technology-demonstrations are of particular importance for establishing and sustaining imaginaries associated with the implementation of new technologies. Since the 1960s they are used to imagine future possibilities of a new media technology. We will not give a full history of this field, as this would be too much. Typical examples are the "mother of all demos", Douglas Engelbarts demonstration of the potentials of computer technology in 1968 (Metz 2008) or the wide and interesting "demo-scene" that developed in 1980s with home computing (Botz 2011; Tasajärvi 2004). Instead, the aim of the text is to provide a case study concerning the media artist group Van Gogh-TV and their project *Piazza virtuale* from 1992. (See for a more detailed discussion of many aspects and ideas of this text Ernst and Schröter 2020; Ernst and Schröter 2021).

In the first two parts, the text sketches the theoretical premises by claiming that an STS-based approach towards the performativity of technology demonstrations can give valuable insights for the discussion of media art. In the third part we will discuss the problem how temporality, imagination and performativity are intertwined in technology demonstrations. The text concludes with an argument regarding the relation between media art and the problem of the 'future' of new media.

2 Sociotechnical Imaginaries and Public Demonstrations of Technology

Imagination was for a long time primarily a topic of literary theory (Iser 1993). Yet, historically it was the difference between images and imagination which sparked most of the philosophical discussions on imagination. The equivocal status of images between a mental image and a material picture was indicative for the fact that imagination is not only a cognitive faculty but also a collective process, associated with specific objects and practices in social reality (Walton 1990). This led to a growing interest in imagination in the social sciences, especially in STS (McNeil 2017) and cultural anthropology (Sneath et al. 2009). Imagination is not only 'in our head' but performed in social practices of presenting and staging objects. Certainly, is it possible to limit the notion of 'imagination' to a personal form of imagination of the individual subject e.g. in cognitive science. But when it comes to the 'meaning' of an imagination it is always necessary to keep a broader understanding. Such a notion of imagination has to include an understanding of a 'collective imaginary' which is shaped by culture and society and which is always already at work when our subjective minds are imagining something.

During the twentieth century various notions of such a collective imaginary were developed, especially in the works of Cornelius Castoriadis, most importantly his book *The Imaginary Institution of Society* (1987, orig. French 1975). Coming from a Marxist perspective and being critical of the psychoanalytic movement of his time, Castoriadis starts from the fact of permanent social change. For Castoriadis, society is a "social-historical institution" (Castoriadis 1987, p. 322) which is intertwined with an undetermined "radical imagination." This "radical imagination" (Castoriadis 1987, p. 142) provides society with the ability to cope with the contingencies of social reality, a "radical otherness" (Castoriadis 1987, p. 172) that society has to face permanently. It's not difficult to adopt this very fundamental philosophical notion of imagination and to apply it to the question how technology is changing society.

Yet, the premise is to understand the imagination of technology in itself as a form of "technology" in the sense of "techniques" of imagination (Sneath et al. 2009). One way to do that is to consider new technologies as embedded in "sociotechnical imaginaries" (Jasanoff and Kim 2015). According to Jasanoff, sociotechnical imaginaries are "[...] collectively held, institutionally stabilized, and publicly performed visions of desirable futures, animated by shared understandings of forms of social life and social order attainable through, and supportive of, advances in science and technology" (Jasanoff 2015a, p. 4). This notion of is focused on the contingencies of technology. Science and technology cause irritations in society which result in a mobilization of the imagination. Narrative genres like Science Fiction have been linked with the imagination of new technologies, e.g. in the field of computers (Ferro and Swedin 2011). However, research in STS is far less interested in the history and aesthetics of Sci-Fi-literature or films themselves but committed to the implications fictional narratives in Sci-Fi have for *factual* discourses: "Technological innovation often follows at the heels of science fiction, lagging authorial imagination by decades or longer" (Jasanoff 2015a, p. 1). This quote by Sheila Jasanoff reflects view on Sci-Fi, as Sci-Fi is usually regarded as 'prophetic' or 'visionary.' Sci-Fi represents without a doubt the avantgarde in imagining future scenarios, as much as Sci-Fi can be 'prophetic,' it can be biased as well, blocking or obfuscating technological possibilities or the search for solutions. Sci-Fi must be seen as part of a "futures industry" (Eshun 2003, p. 290), situating Sci-Fi within a broader context of sociotechnical imaginaries. Thus, for STS, the relations between different forms of imaginaries are of particular interest, e.g. the difference between Sci-Fi and what Jasanoff calls "authorial imagination," the latter being imaginaries or official policies of a company or a nation state towards the certain key technologies such as artificial intelligence or renewable energies.

One key aspect of different forms of imaginaries is their medial realization. While Sci-Fi is a form of narration popularized in fictional literature and movies of various sorts, Jasanoff urges us to widen the focus. As Jasanoff writes (quoted above), sociotechnical imaginaries are realized in "publicly performed visions of desirable futures." This allows us to consider technology-demonstrations and other forms of 'public performing' of new technologies as a form of realizing sociotechnical imaginaries. Just as in the case of fictional representations of new technologies, the reference to a specific object, especially to prototypes, plays a decisive role. In fictional contexts—e.g. the case of the famous gesture-based user-interface in Steven Spielberg's film *Minority Report* (2003) (Kirby 2010, p. 50 ff.)—prototypes for new technologies appear to project a possible future based on real-world concepts for these technologies. STS-scholar David Kirby has called this "diegetic prototypes" (Kirby 2010). In contrast, the objects shown at technology demonstrations are real objects, most of which (but not necessarily) represent technologies that will be marketable in the near future. This reference to the real use of a technology in the near future characterizes technology demonstrations in that they give a 'sample' of a future technology which will soon be available to the general public. Not that the technological object in a technology demonstration is only *possibly* real, as in fictional contexts, but it *is* real. As philosopher Nicholas Rescher (1998, p. 40) has argued, this difference represents the difference between a speculation and a forecast, because only the latter entails a full commitment on the existence of a future state of affairs. Thus, technology demonstrations serve, to use a famous notion by Nelson Goodman, as real-world "exemplifications" of a new technology (Goodman 1968, p. 52 ff.). The technology possesses certain displayed properties and is committed—*via* the performativity of the demonstration—to the existence of an imagined future associated with that technology.

3 Technology-Demonstrations: Displaying Possibilities

The imagination of the future is linked to, often utopian, promises of technological progress. One of the most famous (and most politicized) forms of demonstrating the possibilities of future technologies are the world fairs. Established in the nineteenth century, these exhibitions serve as demonstrations of the power of individual nation states (Kihlstedt 1986). Yet, world fairs are only the tip of the iceberg. They are based on an older tradition of public demonstration of scientific knowledge, especially in the context of experiments and the display of virtuosity (Collins 1988). In the twentieth century, this tradition of demonstrating the functionality of technology is becoming an integral part of corporate culture and thus of everyday professional practice. As Claude Rosental (2013) has argued, a broader understanding of "demonstration" develops which goes hand in hand with a broader understanding of social functions of demonstrations of technology, most importantly with regard to their normative and communicative functions (Rosental 2013, p. 344 ff.). Of the various functions identified by Rosental four are of particular interest in the given context:

1. Constitution of public understandings of technology: technology-demonstrations are intertwined with the constitution of public understanding of technology. They are political because they shape what the public thinks of a certain technology. A public understanding means to bind different actors with very different agencies together (Rosental 2013, p. 345).
2. Constitution of a connection between industry and its markets: technology-demonstrations serve economic purposes, as markets and "micro-markets" are created by the demonstration of successful prototypes; a "binding" between "making and marketing" occurs (Rosental 2013, p. 354).
3. Constitution of exchange between experts: Within groups of experts, most notably scientists and engineers (but artists or military experts as well) technology-demonstrations serve as "transactional devices"; they are "a

medium through which participants could discover new people, institutions, and resources" (Rosental 2013, p. 353 ff.).

4. Constitution of reference points for technology-assessment: To witness a technology-demonstration means to have a "cognitive tool" in order to assess future implications of a technology—be it with regard to possible use cases or with regard of its long-term consequences (Rosental 2013, p. 350). This assessment remains abductive in nature (as nobody knows for certain what the future might hold). Nevertheless, technology-demonstrations serve the purpose to replace speculation (e.g. in Sci-Fi) by evidence-based forms of reasoning; a "measurement" of the technology by the standards of real-world use-cases becomes possible.[1]

Taken together, these four communicative functions provide valuable insights especially into the 'mediality' of technology-demonstrations themselves. Within the context of sociotechnical imaginaries, technology demonstrations help not only to draw the attention of heterogeneous groups of actors to an object, but also to mediate between the interests of these different groups. However, in order to be able to better analyze technology demonstrations in terms of their persuasive power, it is necessary to understand more precisely how the significance of a new technology is framed in the context of such presentations. For this, STS researcher Wally Smith has developed an approach under the heading "Theatre of Use" (Smith 2009). Building on the seminal works by Steven Shapin and Simon Schaffer (Shapin and Schaffer 1985), he identifies the performative aspect of technology-demonstrations as the creation of a moment in which the audience is able to "see for themselves," which is in fact a form of production of (presentative) evidence (Smith 2009, p. 451 ff.). Historically, this "Theatre of Use" is of great importance when it comes to study how a technology or a scientific discovery is accompanied by utopian ideas and ideological frames.

If one takes the notion of 'displaying' a technology literally, this means that in the public demonstration of a scientific experiment not the 'real' scientific experiment is presented, but an *exemplification* of that real experiment; it is, as Wally Smith writes, a "showing of how it might be done" (Smith 2009, p. 453) which refers to the reality of experimenting in everyday practices of science. The same holds true for a demonstration of new technology. When a company like Apple or Tesla presents a new gadget or service, we are instructed to see

---

[1] In Goodman (1968) the term "measurement" is used in order to describe certain functions of symbol systems, e.g. within the context of differentiating "analog" and "digital" symbol systems. We use the term here in a more general sense as a term for evaluation.

for ourselves how great the product is. Yet, we know that this demonstration is not the real use of the particular object but an idealized situation. In both cases a contract between the presenter and its audience is in place, through which the understanding of the object with regard to a 'established' use scenario is suspended while the scenario of a 'possible' use is highlighted. In short, what is on display in technology-demonstrations is not the reality of a technological object as such, but the reality of imagined possibilities of the displayed technological object. In this regard the "diegetic prototypes" differ from the objects shown in technology demonstrations. "Diegetic prototypes" are supposed to stimulate the process of imagining a possible reality of a technology. In contrast, technology demonstrations are supposed to help in imagining the real possibilities of that technology, yet they do so by exemplifying idealized parts of that object.

As Nelson Goodman points out, exemplification gives us a "sample" (Goodman 1968, p. 53) of an object. Certain *present* properties of an object are shown in such a way that *absent* features of the object can be imagined by abduction and conjecture, hence associated and projected onto the object. It is exactly this gap between what you see and what you are supposed to imagine on the basis of what you are seeing, where sociotechnical imaginaries work their magic. In *The imaginary institution of society* Castoriadis makes a brief remark on one of the most important mechanisms of imagination. As an integral part of "radical imagination" he identifies the human ability of "not 'imagining what is not' but imagining/figuring one thing by means of another thing, being able to 'see' in what is what is not there, presenting or presentifying one thing by another thing" (Castoriadis 1987, p. 252). Castoriadis had the ability to see analogies between different objects and think in metaphors in mind. But since Castoriadis was mainly concerned with a social philosophy, we also have consider this seeing "in what is what is not there" and "presenting or presentifying one thing by another thing" as a form of collective social practice. In social reality we are able to use a situation as a model for another situation. This is where Wally Smith brings in sociologist Ervin Goffman (1974). Goffman has called this ability the ability to "reframe" a situation by considering a situation A as another situation B. With regard to Smith's "Theatre of use" this is of the utmost importance (Smith 2009, p. 452 ff.), Yet, what Smith fails to acknowledge in his otherwise very insightful analysis of the practices of technology-demonstrations is the fact that this reframing heavily depends on imagination. As we said, a technology-demonstration is not the actual technology but a demonstration of the 'realities of the possibilities' of that technology. In consequence, the force of a rhetoric operation like "letting the spectators see for themselves" consists in its imaginative temporal reference to a possible future state of affairs.

This process is different from the case of David Kirby's "diegetic prototypes", provided, that e.g. the calls for subsequent action that accompany these types of presentation are also different. In the case of a technology like in a Sci-Fi-Film as *Minority Report*, one might say that it is desirable (or to be feared) to have a certain technology in the future. In the case of technology-demonstrations, however, the call to subsequent action may be that one is asked to use (and buy) the specific technological object. If this distinction can be made on the basis of a classical 'pragmatic' argument, intermediate phenomena between the two forms of demonstrating technology emerge. Media art for example is an interesting case with regard to technology-demonstrations, because it is obviously a practice of displaying media objects, and in many cases *new* media objects, yet it lacks the real-world implications of a product-demonstration.[2] Instead of defining media art at this point, we would like to give an example to illustrate this intermediate status of media art. The example is the project *Piazza virtuale* (1992) by the media artist group Van Gogh-TV.

4 (Re-)Imagining Possible Futures: Television or Internet?

Today more or less forgotten, *Piazza virtuale* was an installment of a fully operational form of interactive television. It was on air for 100-days, broadcasting from the *documenta IX* in Kassel in 1992. The future of media presented in *Piazza virtuale* in 1992 was strongly influenced by the main topics of the time—ideas of interactivity, participation, virtuality and the idea of a new public sphere were all over the place in these days. Usually, these topics were associated with digital media and not television. Nevertheless, while *Piazza virtuale* shares many features with other technology-demonstrations such as the famous "Mother of all demos" by Douglas Engelbart in 1968, its main idea was not to demonstrate the 'computer as a medium' as such (like Engelbart), but the effects of an experimental transformation of an already existing medium. Following the zeitgeist, the project is described in a contemporary documentary as an emancipation of the viewer.[3]

---

[2] Although sometimes media art is especially oriented towards obsolete technologies (Krauss 1999). But that still means that a technology is displayed and 'demonstrated.'

[3] We refer to this documentary because it is one of the few publicly accessible sources for the project. The quotes are from tapes recorded and stored by the artists themselves. The first part of the documentary can be found on YouTube, see https://www.youtube.com/watch?v=xTYWeCvcKzo, last visited 19 May 2020.

In the documentary, *Piazza virtuale* is represented as "another vision of television, in which the viewer is the star of the program, the interactive live TV-program *Piazza virtuale*" (TC 00:01:17)—a "interactive public platform for the television viewer" (TC 00:02:06). The program was broadcasted on workdays 1.5 h via 3sat and 3 h. via Olympus satellite and on weekends 6 h via 3sat and 3 h via satellite. The primary mode of accessing *Piazza virtuale* was by telephone, but one could also use modems, FAX or picture phones. As the documentary explains, "there are 20 telephone lines which connect viewers with each other via the central computer, enabling them to communicate with each other live on the air. The response was overwhelming. There were more than 110.000 callers every hour" (TC 00:03:44). While the idea to break up the one-directional public sphere created by television through more 'interactive' represents one of the leading ideas for 'new media' in the late 1980s and early 1990s is portrayed quite well in the documentary, one has to be aware of the fact that the documentary is not only a 'reframing' (in the sense of Wally Smith and Ervin Goffman) of the performative demonstration itself, but an attempt to "remediate" (Bolter and Grusin 2000) the medium television with the help of digital technology (Fig. 1).

Following the concept of the project, the future of television was demonstrated by letting the users discover the possibilities of interaction for themselves. *Piazza virtuale* was the promise to demonstrate a new form of public sphere, different from the established dominance of television over public discourse. The idea of letting the viewers "see for themselves" what is possible was supposed to be achieved through participation. However, participation is problematic in that it presupposes that users know what they have to do. In order to become self-determined users who can fulfil the high ideals of the technological utopia of transgressing the boundaries of the traditional public spheres created by television, users must first be familiarized with the interfaces that enable them to interact. For this reason, *Piazza virtuale* provided a tutorial called "school". Comparable to interactive tutorials for software such as computer games or office programs, the users learned how to use the telephone as an interface. This concerned in particular multimedia gimmicks such as the possibility of making music or painting pictures together. But the phenomenon as such is interesting as well. It shows that very different user groups interacted 'virtually' in the context of *Piazza*. While those who dialed in with videophones or modems were undoubtedly part of the technical avantgarde at the time, already using the internet and being able to chat on the *Piazza*, the use of the telephone as an interactive access and control medium via the television set was new (Figs. 2 and 3).

To consider being on the *Piazza* as being "online" is interesting. Certainly, this was an obvious name, yet it underscores the idea, alluded to in such terms

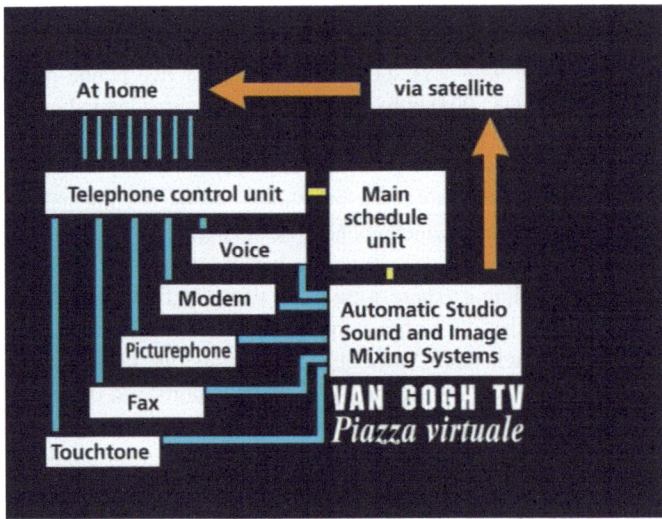

Fig. 1 Representation of the different ways to access *Piazza virtuale*. *Source*: Screenshot from Van Gogh TV, *Piazza virtuale*, "The Documentation" (1992), (Material of the DFG project "Van Gogh TV. Multimedia Documentation and Analysis of their Legacy", Prof. Anja Stöffler, Prof. Dr. Jens Schröter, Tape 461, Box 37, date 01.03.93)

as 'cyberspace', that digital media lead to a kind of integration into a different 'space' generated by computers. Being "online" was the condition for participation in the virtual space of the *Piazza*. The decisive difference to notions of being "online" in the WWW was in this case the double function of the telephone. In order to go "online" on the *Piazza* the telephone was the primary access medium. In contrast to the WWW, however, not only computers could be connected via the telephone, but the telephone itself could be used as a medium for interactive input in addition to conversations without having to use a computer. A touch-tone interface was used for this purpose, which also turned the telephone into a haptic medium for interaction. The telephone and the oral language—and not the keyboard as in 'Internet Relay Chats'—were seen as the primary medium to connect heterogeneous groups with each other in the framework of a live broadcast. A core-problem of the project here was the limited number of communications, which could not be realized as clearly separated, discrete communication. Speaking in disarray live on air was confusing and created a certain cacophony.

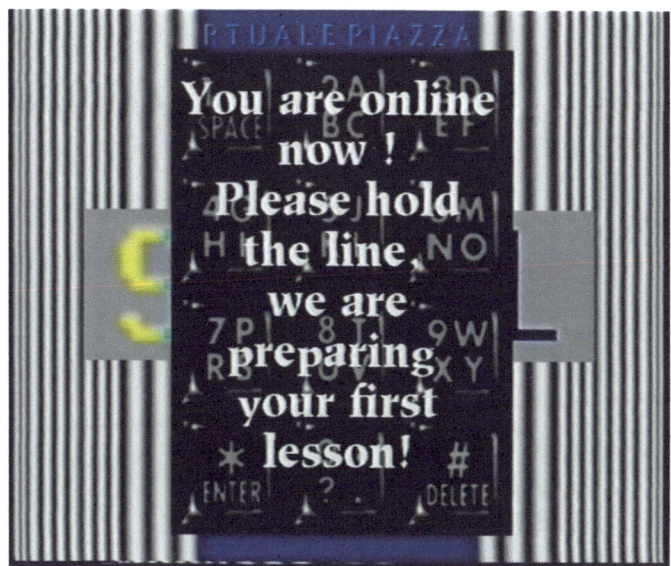

Fig. 2 Start screen of the tutorial of *Piazza virtuale*. *Source*: Screenshot from Van Gogh TV, *Piazza virtuale*, "The Documentation" (1992), Material of the DFG project "Van Gogh TV. Multimedia Documentation and Analysis of their Legacy", Prof. Anja Stöffler, Prof. Dr. Jens Schröter, Tape 1, Box 1, date 13 June 1992

Given this transformation of the telephone into a digital access tool, one could ask if *Piazza virtuale* was not so much about reinventing the television as "interactive television" but and foremost about digitization of the media sphere in itself. Intended to demonstrate how interactive Television works, the project demonstrated the 'reality of possibilities' of the digitization of another medium as such. Instead of following the interpretation provided by the documentary one can ask: whose and which possibilities were actually demonstrated? Was the project about the possibilities of television or was it about the possibilities of some other medium, a medium which was in 1992 not yet fully realized, not yet fully imaginable? To put it more pointedly: was *Piazza virtuale* about a new medium in the sense of a "remediated" (Bolter and Grusin 2000)—that is: reframed and thus reimagined—television? Or was it about experimenting with technological possibilities which transcended television? Was this 'other' medium only expressed by using the 'frame' of the old medium television? Did *Piazza virtuale* only appear as television but was in reality producing something else, something which is, at

Fig. 3 Tutorial of the touch-tone-interface of *Piazza virtuale*. *Source*: Screenshot from Van Gogh TV, *Piazza virtuale*, "The Documentation" (1992), (Material of the DFG project "Van Gogh TV. Multimedia Documentation and Analysis of their Legacy", Prof. Anja Stöffler, Prof. Dr. Jens Schröter, Tape 1, Box 1, date 13 June 1992)

least form hindsight, much closer to what we today would call a 'social medium' which was based on network-centric communication? (Van Gogh TV 2020).

The documentary establishes the frame that *Piazza virtuale* was about, as it is put in the film, a "new vision of television"—that this is the future which is implied. But we have to be aware that there is a small but very important difference between the *reality of possibilities* and a *possible future reality*. As the field of Futures Studies remind us (Rescher 1998), every demonstrated reality of possibilities holds different, heterogeneous, antagonistic and conflicting possible future realities. Sociotechnical imaginaries are not only relevant for conceiving a technology in the first place, but for regulating and shaping what we have called here the reality of possibilities as well.

The TV-Documentary gives us one imaginary, the idea of a reinvention of television. In this future scenario, digital technology is used to "remediate" television and to 'reframe' the understandings of the public sphere. But there is also a *different* imaginary, in which television is used to reframe digital technology, to 'socialize' digital technology in ways it has not yet been done before, although, and these are the contingencies of what Castoriadis considers as the "indetermined" dynamics of the "social-historical," Tim Berners-Lee and others were working on at that time. And there is the problem of 're-imagining' those older visions. The dualistic view with television on one side and the WWW on the other side might, from hindsight, not suffice. Media art might have demonstrated in the case of *Piazza virtuale* the possibility of the third itself, a hybrid medium, neither television nor WWW. The question is: can we imagine this 'third medium' without considering *Piazza virtuale* as a new form of television nor as an early form of social media?

5 Conclusion

Analogies are great and indispensable heuristic tools. Certainly, the analogy to social media is tempting and up to a certain point very plausible. This doesn't come as a surprise as analogies are based on perceived similarities between something very familiar like social media of today and something which seems like a strange project in a strange time. Nevertheless, epistemology and historiography taught over and over again to be skeptical not of the use of heuristic use of analogies as such, but of their validity. Thus, working with analogies one is obliged to question our assumptions and results. To put it a little bit provocative: what if one is, given our point in time, just wanting to imagine *Piazza virtuale* as an early forerunner of social media? This wouldn't be surprising, as perceived analogies are always filled with imagination. But is there a good reason to be skeptical?

If one would consider the legacy of a project like *Piazza virtuale* in a literal sense as a precursor of social media, then there are good reasons to be skeptical. The idea and the whole struggle behind *Piazza virtuale* seem to have been to open up the communication regime of traditional mass media, to allow for performance in the sense of spontaneous communication, to empower the individual. In this sense, the participatory aspect of *Piazza virtuale* holds resemblance to social media. But there are problems as well, as *Piazza virtuale* does not share many of the core features of social networks of today. Most importantly, it lacked the databases to profile the users as it was invented within the limits of a technology-demonstration as a *spontaneous* medium, borrowing from television the "liveness" and combining it with new possibilities provided by digitization of technologies at the time. Does this mean, the analogy is wrong? Not necessarily, but from a methodological standpoint one has to be aware of its limitations. *Piazza virtuale* is a precursor of social media, but as an aesthetic idea of a relation between media and sociality, as, in a positive way, a performative deconstruction of mass media. In this sense, *Piazza virtuale* set free imaginations of alternative sociality *via* the performative transformation of the mass media of its time. However, what is decisive here is something quite different. The fact that a technology demonstration like *Piazza virtuale* is interpreted about 40 years later as a precursor form of social media shows very clearly that the initial premise to link technology-demonstrations with sociotechnical imaginaries is correct. The process of associating a specific future with the objects demonstrated in technology demonstrations is never complete and can be never complete. What is in fact changing are rather the "sociotechnical imaginaries" which frame these futures. What was celebrated in 1990 as the reinvention of television is now read as a precursor form of social media. Hence, what has really changed are the imaginaries with which we interpret a technology that is demonstrated to us.

References

Bolter, Jay D., and R.A. Grusin. 2000. *Remediation. Understanding new media.* Cambridge: The MIT Press.
Botz, Daniel. 2011. *Kunst, Code und Maschine. Die Ästhetik der Computer-Demoszene.* Bielefeld: transcript.
Castoriadis, Cornelius. 1987. *The imaginary institution of society.* Cambridge: Polity.
Collins, Harry M. 1988. Public experiments and displays of virtuosity: The core-set revisited. *Social Studies of Science* 18: 725–748.
Ernst, Christoph, and Jens Schröter. 2021. Die Zukunft vorstellen – Technologie-Demonstrationen in der Geschichte digitaler Medien. *Technikgeschichte* 88 (1): 79–105.
Ernst, Christoph, and Jens Schröter. 2020. *Zukünftige Medien. Eine Einführung.* Wiesbaden: Springer VS.
Eshun, Kodwo. 2003. Further considerations of Afrofuturism. *The New Centennial Review* 3: 287–302.
Ferro, David L., and E.G. Swedin, eds. 2011 S. *Science fiction and computing. Essays on interlinked domains.* Jefferson: McFarland & Company.
Goffman, Erving. 1973. *The presentation of self in everyday life.* Woodstock: Overlook Press.
Goffman, Erving. 1974. *Frame analysis: An essay on the organization of experience.* Cambridge: Harvard University Press.
Goodman, Nelson, et al. 1968. *Languages of art. An approach to a theory of symbols.* Indianapolis: Bobbs-Merrill.
Iser, Wolfgang. 1993. *The fictive and the imaginary. Charting literary anthropology.* Baltimore: Johns Hopkins University Press.
Jasanoff, Sheila. 2015a. Future imperfect. Science, technology, and the imagination of modernity. In *Dreamscapes of modernity. Sociotechnical imaginaries and the fabrication of power,* ed. S. Jasanoff and S.-H. Kim, 1–33. Chicago: University of Chicago Press.

Jasanoff, Sheila. 2015b. Imagined and invented worlds. In *Dreamscapes of modernity. Sociotechnical imaginaries and the fabrication of power*, ed. S. Jasanoff and S.-H. Kim, 321–341. Chicago: University of Chicago Press.

Jasanoff, Sheila, and Sang-Hyun Kim, eds. 2015. *Dreamscapes of modernity. Sociotechnical imaginaries and the fabrication of power*. Chicago: University of Chicago Press.

Kihlstedt, Folke T. 1986. Utopia realized. The world fairs of the 1930s. In *Imagining tomorrow. History, technology, and the American future*, ed. Joseph Corn, 97–118. Cambridge: The MIT Press.

Kirby, David A. 2010. The future is now: Diegetic prototypes and the role of popular films in generating real-world technological development. *Social Studies of Science* 40: 41–70.

Krauss, Rosalind E. 1999. Reinventing the medium. *Critical Inquiry* 25: 289–305.

McNeil, Maureen, et al. 2017. Conceptualizing imaginaries of science, technology, and society. In *The handbook of science and technology studies*, ed. Ulrike Felt, 435–463. Cambridge: The MIT Press.

Metz, Cade. 2008. The Mother of All Demos – 150 years ahead of its time. Theregister.co.uk. https://www.theregister.co.uk/2008/12/11/engelbart_celebration/. Accessed 11 May 2020.

Rescher, Nicholas. 1998. *Predicting the future. An introduction to the theory of forecasting*. Albany: State University of New York Press.

Rosental, Claude. 2013. Toward a sociology of public demonstrations. *Sociological Theory* 31: 343–365.

Shapin, Steven, and Simon Schaffer. 1985. *Leviathan and the air-pump. Hobbes, Boyle, and the experimental life*. Princeton: Princeton University Press.

Smith, Wally. 2009. Theatre of use: A frame analysis of information technology demonstrations. *Social Studies of Science* 39: 449–480.

Sneath, David, M. Holbraad, and M.A. Pedersen. 2009. Technologies of the imagination: An introduction. *Ethos*. https://doi.org/10.1080/00141840902751147.

Tasajärvi, Lassi. 2004. *Demoscene: The art of real-time*. Helsinki: Even Lake Studios.

Van Gogh TV. 2020. Ein Forschungsprojekt an der Hochschule Mainz und der Rheinischen Friedrich-Wilhelms-Universität Bonn. https://vangoghtv.hs-mainz.de. Accessed 19 May 2020.

Walton, Kendall L. 1990. *Mimesis as make-believe. On the foundations of the representational arts*. Cambridge: Harvard University Press.

Televisionen/Television/Televisuality/ Televirtuality. Imaginary of TV in the 1980s and 1990s

Oliver Fahle

Abstract

This text unfolds three arguments about the relation between television and imagination. Every argument has a different focus: The first systematic argument claims that television is based on a deep ambiguity: it constantly moves between artistic imagination on the one hand, and, on the other, the notion of a domestic medium that only represents the ordinary reality of everyday life. The second historical argument follows the assumption that this ambiguity, or difference, ended in the middle of the 1980s and was replaced by a new thinking about television as an opening of new layers of the imaginary. The third epistemological argument will give a proposal about what this new way of thinking about television may implicate regarding the concept of virtuality. The discussion develops along the four concepts in the title of this paper, which serve to describe different expectations for television.

Keywords

Television • Virtuality • Media Theory

1 The Ambiguity of Television

Television is an ambiguous construct in respect to an idea of the imaginary: On the one hand it is a medium that has generated a multitude of expectations and

O. Fahle (✉)
Institut für Medienwissenschaft, Ruhr-Universität Bochum, Bochum, Germany
E-Mail: oliver.fahle@rub.de

© The Author(s), under exclusive license to Springer Fachmedien Wiesbaden GmbH, part of Springer Nature 2021
C. Ernst and J. Schröter (eds.), *(Re-)Imagining New Media*, Neue Perspektiven der Medienästhetik, https://doi.org/10.1007/978-3-658-32899-3_5

Fig. 1 Cover Peter Paul Kubitz: Der Traum vom Sehen and Claus Eurich/Gerd Würzburg: 30 Jahre Fernsehalltag. *Source*: Kubitz 1997; Eurich and Würzburg 1983

imaginations. On the other hand, no other type of popular media is associated in such a way with social fear and manipulation of the public and individual knowledge. This can be demonstrated by two book titles from the 1980s (Fig. 1).

First, we are going to have a look at the book title on the left side. We see a catalogue of an exhibition that took place in the Gasometer in Oberhausen in 1987 that explored an old idea linked to different optical media, insisting particularly on the significance of television (Kubitz 1997). It was called "Televisionen: Der Traum vom Sehen" (English: "Televisions: The Dream of Seeing") and explores various ideas and concepts in art and science to realize that dream. There is no adequate translation for the German term "Televisionen" in English: It comprises the plural of television but also the plural of vision. Therefore, "Televisionen" (keeping the German term for the moment) emphasizes three ideas of television: first, the term "tele", which means: "far" or "far from" or "distant"; second, the term "vision", meaning: "to see"; third, the term "visionen" (visions), indicating the meaning: to see more than the actual vision of reality can provide.

Thus, thinking of Television(en) always implies an idea of (the) imaginary even if often neglected by the discourse on television. The book by Kubitz is one of the first of various exhibitions and catalogues of the 1980 and 1990s in

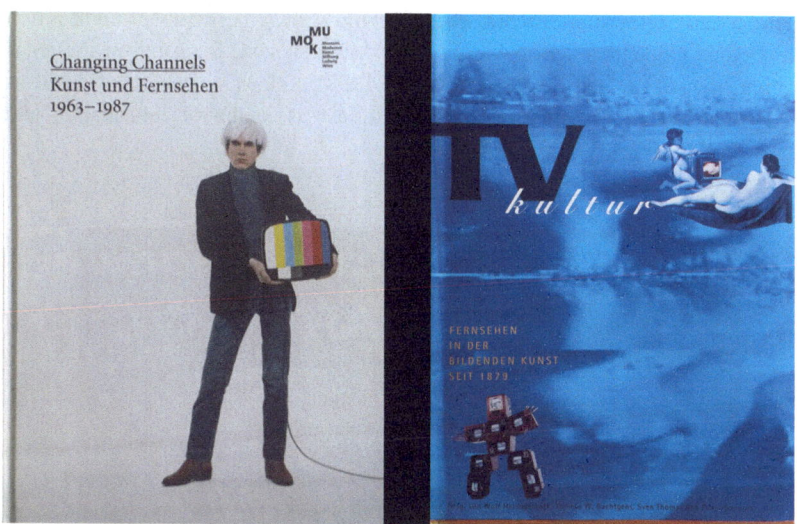

Fig. 2 Cover Mumok: Changing Channels and Wulf Herzogenrath: TV-Kultur. *Source*: Mumok 2010; Herzogenrath et al. 1997

Germany, dealing with aspects of the television's imaginary. In the following years there have been even more projects exploring this territory of art and television (Herzogenrath et al. 1997; Mumok 2010; Fig. 2).

These catalogues compile works of art from the 1960s and 1970s who engaged with television in various ways. The collections emphasize the importance of television as a medium for inspiration or imagination. Many examples are grounded in a belief of a higher mission or greater potential of television. In a way, these artworks can be understood as precursors to the *Piazza virtuale*-Project and Van Gogh TV. They consider television not only as an apparatus but as a complex dispositive that is able to go beyond its function as domestic information and entertainment device. *Piazza virtuale* tended to create a new and large platform of communication, following several ideas that artists already developed in the 1960s and 1970s. This period seems to be the most promising time when it comes to understanding the hopes and possibilities linked to television as a medium of 'true experience' of reality. In sum, these would constitute the notion of "Televisionen", the first term linked to the imaginary, highlighting the aspect of "vision".

Let us briefly look at some of these projects from the 1960s and '70s:

In an early television artwork, Gerry Schum shows the works of eight artists like Dennis Oppenheim, Bob Smithson or Mike Heizen, focusing on the overlapping of land art and television (Kubitz 1997). Television was considered as an active actor in the creation of art, not just as media of information and representation of art (Fig. 3).

Fig. 3 Gerry Schum: Fernsehgalerie 1969/1970. *Source*: Kubitz 1997, p. 29

The tension between the artists' engagement with landscape and the framing and intervention of the television image creates the center of these works. Schum's project can be considered as one of the various artworks aiming to extend the possible experience of television that took place in the late 1960s and early 1970s. Artists began to explore theses potentials that could already be found in the technical and dispositive conditions. Inspired by McLuhan's idea that television is a cool medium (McLuhan 1994, pp. 22 ff.) which requires the viewing or hearing experience to complete the medium's message, TV was conceived as a possible open space for vision, communication and democratic exchange.

A large number of these artists pursued creative experiments using the technical materiality of television like Nam June Paik's "Global Groove" (1973), Steina and Woody Vasulska's "Sketches" (1970) or, as an early representation, Wolf Vostell's "Sun in your head" (1963). All these examples comprehend television as an experimental place to create another way of seeing, often by interrupting the process of transmission and by deconstructing the transparency of the television image as a fixed entity. Instead of the classical representation, these works depict a constant variation and a permanent modification of technical and perceptual changes and passages.

These are only a few examples showing that there was a great potential of what television could be as a matter of imagination, especially for the 1970s. However, this raises the question if, eventually, this potential refers to other media displays or configuration of moving images, namely that of video and video art. Artists in that period who looked for the potential of television began to keep an eye on video which was technically similar to television, but had the advantage of individual handling and appeared as a fresh medium for an upcoming electronic and digital era. Either way, these art works at least dealt with the interface of television and video, considering the potential of electronic media in a crossover between different screens and displays. I would argue that the early 1970s qualify to be the golden age of the encounter of art and television.

At the same time, there is yet the other side of television. Peter Paul Kubitz, the organizer of the exhibition in the Gasometer, summarizes this in an interview with Alexander Kluge:

"These are Dutch telescopes used by an Italian physicist and writer in order to, for instance, observe Jupiter's moons. However, television has significantly departed from that purpose; essentially, it serves as a mere reference on cultural history to which the exhibition alludes. Television itself is more profane. In my opinion, television has little to do with the notion of "tele-vision," i.e., seeing far. Neither does it come with the gusto of the Columbian discovery. Television is rather simple, yet, in its simplicity, no less fascinating."[1]

Kubitz refers to the ordinary part of television: its simplicity (in German: "Schlichtheit"), which is still very appealing. I suggest to call this other, more ordinary side, simply television (contrasting the term "Televisionen", which accentuates the aspect of art in television).

The book "30 Jahre Fernsehalltag: Wie das Fernsehen unser Leben verändert hat" ("30 years of everyday life television". How television changed our life" (right side of Fig. 1)) by Claus Eurich and Gerd Würzburg (1983) represents this ordinary side of television. The title from 1980 focuses critically on television as a medium of ordinary life and deals with the modification of the family and its communication structure. The difference between the "dream of seeing (far)" and "everyday life television" ('Fernsehalltag') tells a lot about the divergent projections and mental constructions referring to television. Whereas Kubitz's book conveys a promise of a new era of seeing and perception, the study by Eurich and Würzburg wants us to acknowledge the destruction of the family by means of empirical studies of domestic life in Germany in the 1980s.

This difference can be exemplified by contrasting two central pictures of each book. At the end of the exhibition in the Gasometer, Kubitz (the organizer) confronts the spectator with a vision of space and the travel of images taken by the space probes Voyager 1 and Voyager 2 and their trip beyond the limits of our galaxy (lasting at least 40 thousand years) (Fig. 4).

The visual conquest of space is the greatest dream of seeing and the ultimate definition of "Televisionen". That is the reason why the definition of "Televisionen" is to see, with or through ones own body, the most disembodied picture of the world ever. We cannot leave our own body but, we can extend our ways of seeing. Images of space from Voyager to Space Hubble are expressions of this desire to reach the highest point of externalization and disembodiment. It is a real vision or even a hallucination project. And it is the absolute contrast to the way of seeing in everyday life television.

---

[1] Peter Paul Kubitz: "Das sind holländische Fernrohre, die von einem italienischen Physiker und Literaten benutzt wurden, um zum Beispiel Jupitermonde zu sehen. Davon hat sich das Fernsehen selbst aber weiter entfernt, das ist im Grund nur ein rein kulturgeschichtlicher Verweis, auf den die Ausstellung anspielt. Das Fernsehen ist profaner. Aus meiner Sicht hat das Fernsehen mit Ferne relative wenig zu tun, es ist ein kulturgeschichtliches Alltagsmittel. Es hat auch nicht den Gout der kolumbianischen Entdeckung. Es ist schlichter und in dieser Schlichtheit nicht minder faszinierend." (Kluge and Kubitz 1999, p. 40, my translation).

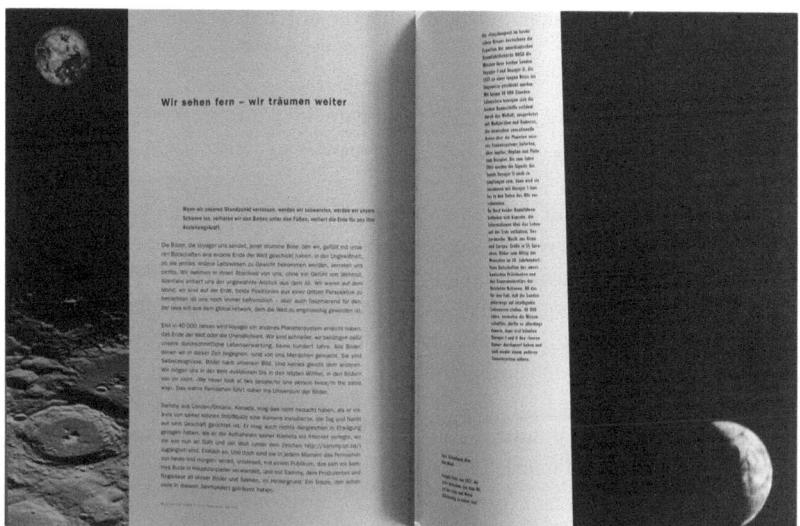

Fig. 4 Der Traum vom Sehen: We look far—we go on dreaming. *Source*: Kubitz 1997, p. 200

Conversely, the cover of the book by Eurich and Würzburg points to the popular side of television, not "Televisionen" but "television". Popular television did not go far beyond the alleged 'normal' or 'ordinary' life, showing directly the TV set in the picture, conceiving itself as a medium of social reality and serving as an apparently transparent window to an upcoming information society. This everyday life television is first and foremost associated with privacy and family life. The cover shows a photograph of a father talking to his children. Even the dog seems to take part in the discussion whereas, interestingly, the mother is absent. The photo centralizes the father because his patriarchal authority is at risk. In fact, the center of the family is transferred from father to television. The gaze of the children is directed much more to the screen than to him, showing that he is already losing control in the family cosmos. It is entirely in that sense that Eurich and Würzburg present several studies which confirm the danger of television to the traditional family.

I would argue that in this contrast between "Televisionen" as a vision of seeing on the one hand, and television as a potential dangerous medium of everyday life, ready to destroy traditional domestic structures, lies a fundamental ambiguity in the discourse about television. Schematically, the differences can be visualized as two poles:

| Televisionen | : imagination | potential | dreaming | outer space | world |
| Television | : reality | real/social | manipulation | inner space | living room |

Given this divergence of the discourses about television, I want to assume that until the 1980s/1990s television was considered either as a medium of dreaming and imagination, or as a simple medium of ordinary life with the tendency to endanger traditional forms of society. But this divergence is itself a product of the discourse about television. This discourse is running through a deep transformation in the 1980s/1990s, loosing gradually its importance or even coming to an end. Looking at this transformation is part of my second chapter, where I want to unfold the historical argument and ask about what happened to the relation between imagination and television.

2 New Layers of Television Through Historical Changes

The 'split-picture' of the ambiguity of television is itself a form of discursive or academic imagination. It is part of what Bill Nichols (1992) calls "epistephilia" which has a "strong effect on our social imagination and sense of cultural identity" (Nichols 1992, p. 178). So, the desire for epistephilia—the pleasure in knowing—also nourished the artistic work and academic discourse of television. This academic attitude puts television in a passive position as a type of medium that is not able to generate its own forms of thinking.

My argument is, that from the 1980s on television was no longer only an object of theory and discursive fantasy but achieved the position of a subject of discourse as well. The expression "subject of discourse" may be misleading because it is difficult to apply the term subject to a medium. It seems, however, that television passed through a process of emancipation from artistic visions on the one hand, and the accusation of social manipulation on the other hand. From then on, television reached much more confidence as a "media player" and as an agent of knowledge and epistemology. This can be exemplified again through visual depiction (Fig. 5):

Marie Winn's (1985) classical study from 1977 is (one of the many) massive attacks on television, its effect on the health of our children and a symbol for the general fear of media. Barry Dutter's (2000) picture from 1993, however, demonstrates the opposite, the new cool significance of television. It became the

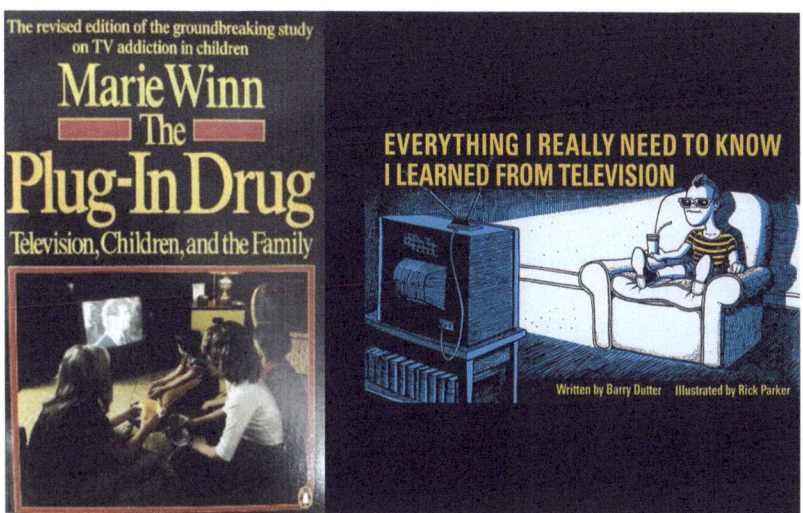

Fig. 5 Cover Marie Winn: The Plug-In Drug: and Barry Dutter: Everything I really need to now I learned it from television (Winn 1985; Dutter 2000)

new transmitter to the world, far from being projected in a utopian or critical way. It is in a way an illustration of Niklas Luhmann's (2000) famous and often quoted beginning of "The Reality of the Mass Media" (Luhmann 2000, p. 1): "Whatever we know about our society, or indeed about the world in which we live, we know from mass media" (he wrote "mass media" but he clearly meant "television"). This sentence of Luhmann is quoted repeatedly, not only because it revealed an absolutely new knowledge about television in 1996, but also because the sovereign coolness with which Luhmann opened his book meant a breakthrough for thinking or speaking about television. Not everyone could have dared to do this with the same sense of nonchalance. If we have a look at the table of contents of the aforementioned book by Wulf Herzogenrath and others about "TV-Kultur. Fernsehen in der Bildenden Kunst seit 1879", which reflects on the relation between television and art works in the course of history, we can identify the following chapters:

The book classifies the 1960s as: "Die Kritik an der TV-Kultur" and the 1970s: "Die Politisierung (politicization) der TV-Kultur". Both headings confirm the observation that TV has been considered as a highly politized and criticized medium of mass communication.

However, this changed in the 1980s. Then, we can read: "The generation of TV kids." (Herzogenrath et al. 1997, p. 5). We easily recognize the adoption of a different stance: neither criticism nor politics, but a new generation of "TV Kids" that is announcing a postmodern approach to the fact of television. The title not only avoids the term of politics and criticism and makes no allusion to either the dream of seeing or to what we have called "Televisionen", but it reveals a new relation to esthetics and epistemology in respect to television.

This new epistemological and esthetical authority that television achieved in the 1980s, was reflected upon in many academic texts in the 1990s. We can mention Umberto Eco's (1985) "Television. La transparence perdu", one of the first texts dealing with the change of television, inspiring another essential text by Francesco Casetti and Roger Odin (1990) in which they further develop the terms "Paleo- and Neotelevision", introduced by Umberto Eco before. We also should not forget Stanley Cavell's (1982) essay about "The fact of television" and, finally, the big volume about the differences of old zero-degree style television and new style television by John Thornton Caldwell (1995) called "Televisuality". Whereas Televisionen/television serve for the imagination of TV for the 1960s/1970s, Televisuality was the appropriate term for the 1980s/1990s.

Caldwell's title focuses on television as a media of constant modification that unfolds anti-causal relations between aesthetic innovation, economic power, technical implementation and the constant modelling of the spectator who from now on is an important factor of televisual production. Televisuality is deeply embedded in these power relations and affective economies and is no longer a simple instrument for manipulation or a display for dreaming. According to Caldwell, Televisuality can be identified by three layers of change: First, there is the aesthetical level, visible above all in the use of video aesthetics in TV programs like MTV or serial formats like "Miami Vice". Second, there is the perceptual change, evident in the invention of the remote control and the possibility to change channels, allowing to switch between alternative worlds, ways of storytelling, iconographies and visual appearances. Third, there is the change of information politics and the general representation of reality transforming profoundly from the 1980s on, exemplified by channels like CNN.

In the 1990s, Televisuality stood or a new self-conscious attitude of television that aesthetically and epistemologically defines (along with other art media) the state of the art. It produces its own imaginary that is no longer projected from the outside by academic discourse of vision and manipulation. Eventually, this opens up an area for a new discussion that I want to define as the fourth term of the imaginary of television: Televirtuality.

3 Neotelevision: From Televisuality to Televirtuality

What does it mean to talk about virtuality in the context of television? The first impression is that virtuality, in a way, bypasses the medium of television. In the middle of the 1990s, the discussion about virtuality circles around cinema and digitization, but not so much about television. In the realm of cinema, Gilles Deleuze's books about the philosophy of cinema and the genealogy of cinematographic images argue that the evolution of modern cinema is completely linked to the time-image (Deleuze 1991). According to Deleuze, modern cinema produces an image unfolding various temporal layers at the same time. Past, present and future come together in a paradoxical—or "crystalized", as Deleuze calls it—figuration and constitute a sort of indecisiveness of different time layers.

Whereas the virtual was an important concept in cinema—at least if we follow a Deleuzian conception of time—it unfolded a first broad discussion in respect to new technologies and the digital. Regarding television, it was first and foremost Jean Baudrillard who developed a theory of the virtual. But the discussion evolving from Baudrillard was completely dominated by his definition of simulation, neglecting its connection to his specific (but less prominent) concept of virtuality. Simulation means, in a very short definition, that we can no longer distinguish between what is 'real' and what is 'image'. Baudrillard has never argued that there is no difference between the real and media, but that we have no possibility to distinguish between them. This is a little but crucial difference. When Baudrillard wrote in three famous texts in 1991: "The gulf war did not take place", he did not want to say that there was no gulf war at all. The French and the English title apprehend it quite precisely: The war had no place (Il n' y avait pas de lieu). It was a somewhat placeless event or a prevented event (to express the paradox linguistically) (Baudrillard 1995).

Hence, Baudrillard did not deny that there was a gulf war (or something that we call so). He did not deny that there was war, dead bodies and destruction. But he was wondering what happened with these evidences as they were constantly transferred into images. It is precisely this shift that he was interested in, and which he would call the 'passage' from the actual to the virtual. As Baudrillard puts it: "The most widespread belief is in a logical progression from virtual to actual, according to which no available weapon will not one day be used and such a concentration of force cannot but lead to conflict. However, this is an Aristotelian logic which is no longer our own. Our virtual has definitively overtaken the actual and we must be content with this extreme virtuality which, unlike the Aristotelian, deters any passage to action. We are no longer in a logic of the passage from virtual to actual but in a hyperrealist logic of the deterrence of the real by the virtual" (Baudrillard 1995, p. 27).

Here, imagination comes into play. The cultural logic of television determines that the passage from virtual to actual is cut off. There is no original link from virtual to actual because television is not a window to reality anymore. For Baudrillard, this marks the end of imagination, since imagination for him is produced by the open space between sign and reality (that he identified in media like baroque art or Graffiti). Television eradicates every body-based sign where the spectator can interact and intervene. There is no "taking place" in Neotelevision, nobody and nothing can "take a place".

In certain aspects, Baudrillard's position is confirmed by other theories of Neotelevision. The already mentioned text by Umberto Eco "TV: Transparency lost" from 1985 defended the idea that Neotelevision is totally concentrating on itself. The former idea that it could be a window to the world or an appropriate representation of the social world finds its end when television only speaks about itself, yet pretends that it deals with the real world in order to do so. Baudrillard's theories analyze correctly the self-referentialization of television in the 1990s.

But why should this self-referentialization necessarily cut off the relation to reality? Perhaps it makes more sense to assume that there is no disappearance of reality but a shift in terms of how we describe and understand reality? If we put it, like Baudrillard, in terms of simulation, we can hardly explore this theoretical direction any further, because by adhering to the term of simulation, there is no way out of the contradiction between reality and sign. Instead of involving simulation, it seems more productive to understand reality in television as a new arrangement of possibilities. Televisuality gives just more options to capture, to form and to represent reality, and it generates more models to visualize it. For Baudrillard, this is synonymous to a "drifting away" from reality—but it is not. It simply makes available more options of reality. Therefore, reality and representation turn into a constant negotiation of how reality could be perceived. We can call these forms of exchange 'virtuality', as Pierre Lévy puts it in 1995: "Virtualization is not a derealization but a mutation of identity, a displacement of the centre of the ontological gravity of the object in consideration. Instead of defining itself first and foremost through its actuality (a 'solution'), the entity henceforth finds its essential consistence in a problematic field (…) Actualization passes from a problem to a solution whereas virtualization passes from a given solution to (another) problem" (Lévy 1995, p. 16). For Lévy, the virtual is not a hidden actual or a possibility of the actual, but it is the response to the actual: a response that reveals another dimension of reality requiring new responses not simply covert in that given reality. Televirtuality expresses this oscillation between visual worlds and its different versions of reality. This does not mean that there is no reality anymore.

The permanent passages between the real and the virtual open up spaces for imagination. Based on this definition, 'imaginary' would not designate the contrast to a material reality, but a shifting activity between the real and the virtual. This differs from older concepts of the image and its metaphors like window, frame or mirror, and yield newer concepts like the virtual or the display, like Francesco Casetti puts it: "The display shows, but only in the sense that it places at our disposition or makes accessible. It exhibits but does not uncover; it offers, but does not commit (...). The display simply makes present images. It places them in front of us, in case we may want to make use of them. It hands them to us, if you will" (Casetti 2015, p. 168).

Taking a last example, a TV magazine that was wholly innovative in the 1990s: BRUT, produced by the channel ARTE, was a pure image program without any form of verbal commentary. It showed images of everything, above all the residue of official images, footage that did not make it into the main program. It presented glimpses 'behind the scenes', scenes of everyday life, everyday people in everyday life, simply let them run. No interpretation, no talking, no context, only a continual production of missing links, output and outtakes going nowhere. In a sense, this innovative format also produced a pure virtual. It produced what I would like to call Televirtuality (Fig. 6).

Thus, reality is not part of a contract or an agreement, but it becomes volatile, an encounter as elusive as our brief contact with the remote control when we switch between different worlds. Like in BRUT, there is always a different reality possible, besides or behind or even into or inside the real. The image does not commit or reveal, it gives space to connect without determining any aspect in the intertwining of technical, aesthetical, communicative and epistemological aspects. The imaginary unfolds only between them.

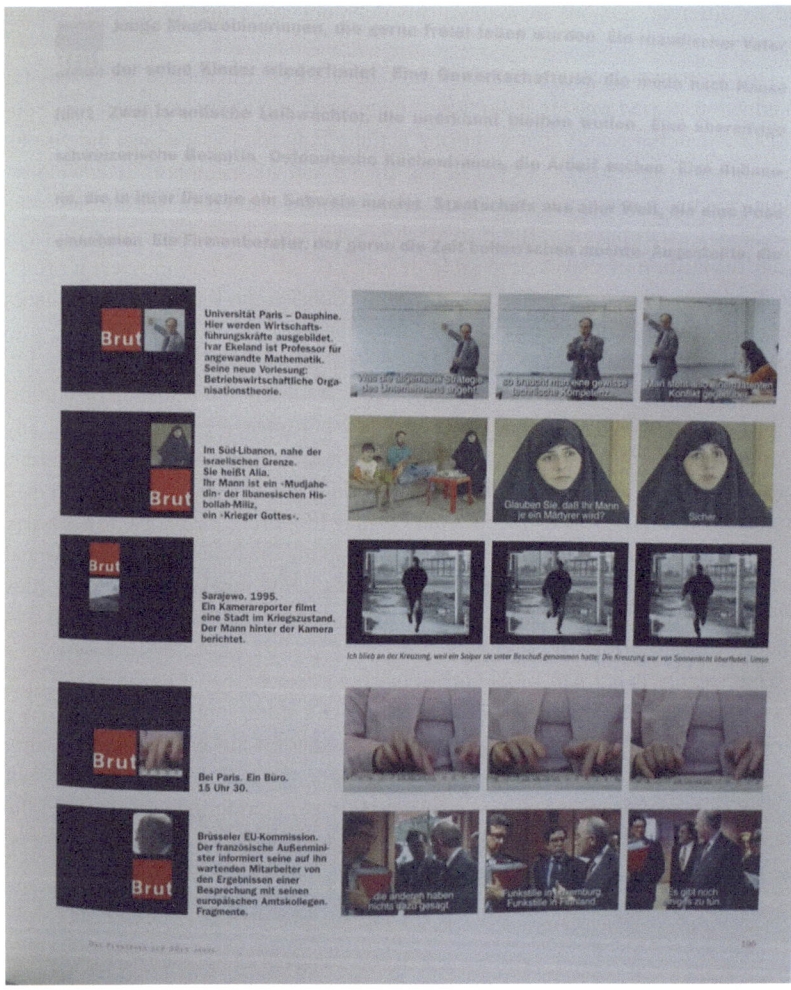

Fig. 6 Brut (Arte). *Source*: Kubitz 1997, p. 196

References

Baudrillard, Jean. 1995. *The Gulf War did not take place*. Bloomington: Indiana University Press (First published in 1991).
Caldwell, John. 1995. *Televisuality. Style. Crisis and authority in American television*. New Brunswick: Rutgers University Press.
Casetti, Francesco, and R. Odin. 1990. De la paléo- à la néotélévision. Approche Sémio-Pragmatique. *Communications* 51: 9–26.
Casetti, Francesco. 2015. *The Lumière Galaxy. 7 keywords for the cinema to come*. New York: Columbia University Press.
Cavell, Stanley. 1982. The fact of television. *Daedalus. Journal of the American Academy of Arts and Sciences* 111 (4): 75–96.
Deleuze, Gilles 1991. *Kino 1. Das Zeit-Bild*. Frankfurt a. M.: Suhrkamp. (First published in 1983)
Dutter, Barry. 2000. *Everything I really need to know I learned from television*. Washington, DC: Applause Theatre and Cinema Books (First published in 1993).
Eco, Umberto. 1985. TV. La transparence perdu. In *La guerre du faux*, ed. Umberto Eco, 196–220. Paris: Grasset.
Eurich, Claus, and G. Würzburg. 1983. *30 Jahre Fernsehalltag. Wie das Fernsehen unser Leben verändert hat*. Reinbek bei Hamburg: Rowohlt.
Herzogenrath, W., T.W. Gaehtgens, S. Thomas, and P. Hoenisch, eds. 1997. *TV-Kultur. Fernsehen in der Bildenden Kunst seit 1879*. Amsterdam: Verlag der Kunst.
Kluge, A., and P.P. Kubitz. 1999. Ein Traum vom Sehen. Ein Gespräch. In *Televisionen*, ed. S. Münker and A. Roesler, 39–53. Frankfurt a. M.: Suhrkamp.
Kubitz, Peter Paul, ed. 1997. *Der Traum vom Sehen. Das Zeitalter der Televisionen*. Dresden: Verlag der Kunst.
Lévy, Pierre. 1995. *Qu'est-ce que le virtuel?* Paris: Éditions la Découverte.
Luhmann, Niklas. 2000. *The reality of the mass media*. Cambridge: Polity (First published in 1996).
McLuhan, Marshall. 1994. *Understanding media. The extension of man*. Massachusetts: MIT Press (First published in 1964).
Museum moderner Kunst Stiftung Ludwig Wien (Mumok), ed. 2010. *Changing Channels – Kunst und Fernsehen 1963–1987*. Köln: Verlag der Buchhandlung Walther König.
Nichols, Bill. 1992. *Representing Reality. Issues and Concepts in Documentary*. Bloomington: Indiana University Press.
Winn, Marie. 1985. *The plug-in drug: Television, children, and the family* (Revised edition). London: Penguin (First published in 1977).

Deconstructing Cyberpunk Worlds—Technodystopian Imaginaries in the Storyworld of Gibson's Neuromancer

Wenzel Mehnert

> "Cyberspace. A consensual hallucination experienced daily by billions of legitimate operators, in every nation, by children being taught mathematical concepts … A graphic representation of data abstracted from the banks of every computer in the human system. Unthinkable complexity. Lines of light ranged in the non space of the mind, clusters and constellations of data. Like city lights, receding." (Gibson 2016, p. 59)

Abstract

Science-Fiction is not only a resource for potentialities of possible futures, but also serves as an archive of past futures and their contemporary reflections on social changes. Within the estranged worlds of the narrations, the authors present the contemporary imaginaries of how society should (or should not) develop in the future. William Gibson's Neuromancer is an important example of this archive. In a dizzyingly detailed description, Gibson depicts a dystopian future dominated by the prevailing irritations and common uncertainties about the future caused by the all-encompassing changes of the 1980s, a decade in which western societies were entering an era of late capitalism with new global market structures and the embedding of new technologies in the everyday life on a unprecedented scale. Within his world Gibson extrapolates the technological potentialities of new and emerging digital technologies like virtual

W. Mehnert (✉)
Universität der Künste Berlin, Berlin, Germany
E-Mail: wenzel.mehnert@udk-berlin.de

© The Author(s), under exclusive license to Springer Fachmedien Wiesbaden GmbH, part of Springer Nature 2021
C. Ernst and J. Schröter (eds.), *(Re-)Imagining New Media*, Neue Perspektiven der Medienästhetik, https://doi.org/10.1007/978-3-658-32899-3_6

reality, artificial intelligence and a digital *Cyberspace*, which is similar to what is today known as the internet, and lays out the implicit sociotechnical imaginaries of his generation. Reciprocally, his novel fostered and distributed the structure of feeling of the '80s on a larger scale, as it became one of the pioneer works of the emerging *Cyberpunk* movement—an influential vision of the future of outgoing twentieth century. This essay is exploring the sociotechnical imaginaries by analyzing the role of new technologies within the power structures of *Neuromancers* storyworld.

Keywords

Sociotechnial Imaginaries • Storyworld • Cyberpunk • Neuromancer • William Gibson • Science Fiction • Futures • Late Capitalism

1   Jacking In

In the year 1984 William Gibson published *Neuromancer*,[1] a Science-Fiction (SF) novel, which revolutionized the genre and offered its readers a glimpse into a world entangled in *Cyberspace*.[2] The book presents a dystopia, which manifested the contemporary fear of technological progress.

Neuromancer is an interesting novel for many reasons. For one, it presents itself as a constant stream of neologisms and novel ideas: Within the story we follow Case, a *console cowboy*,[3] who lives in the *Sprawl*[4] and suffers under the loss of his ability to *jack in* to the *Cyberspace matrix*. He used to be a thief who worked for other thieves and hacked through *ICE*[5] to steal data from big

---

[1] It was his debut novel and also the first novel that won each of the three major awards in SF (Hugo Award, Nebula Award & Philip K. Dick Award).

[2] The term was coined by Gibson and first introduced in a short story called "Burning Chrome" (Gibson 1982).

[3] Console Cowboys stands for an archetype of a hacker.

[4] Officially known as the Boston-Atlanta Metropolitan Axis; an urban area that developed along the east coast of the United States and merges all major cities between Boston and Atlanta. Geodetic domes cover parts of the Sprawl, which hinders the residents from experiencing the natural day-night cycle and the weather. As describe in the fandom glossary of the universe: "Before dawn the geodesics are lightening into gray and then pink" (*"The Sprawl"*), which also explains the famous first lines in the book: "The sky above the port was the color of television, tuned to a dead channel." (Gibson 2016, p. 1).

[5] *Intrusion Countermeasures Electronics* is a spatial firewall that protects sensible data and computer systems: "Ice patterns formed and reformed on the screen as he probed for gaps,

multinational companies called *Zaibatsus*. One day he stole from his employees who, in return, cut his access to the *Cyberspace* by damaging his nervous system. He became "just another hustler, trying to make it through" (Gibson 2016, p. 5).[6] Case is introduced as a morally ambiguous antihero.

Another reason is Gibson's "telling use of detail, its carefully constructed intricacy, its willingness to carry extrapolation into the fabric of daily life" (Sterling 1986, p. xiv). This became the trademark not only for him but also for a whole sub-genre of SF called Cyberpunk.[7] The genre is so strongly influenced by Gibson's writing that some critics even say he is "the one major writer who is original and gifted enough to make the whole movement seem original and gifted." (Csicsery-Ronay 1991, p. 185).

Cyberpunk fictions tell stories of dystopian worlds, which build up on the extrapolations of reality into an imaginary near-future setting. They are depicted through the eyes of Low-Lifes—"disaffected loner[s] from outside the cultural mainstream" (Kelly and Kessel 2007a, p. xi)—like drug addicts, bounty hunters or street gang members. The society they live in is entangled in high technologies of various kinds. Often, the characters are enhanced by cybernetic-implants, connect to the matrix through bodily sensor-stimulations, and interact with human-like A.I.s on an everyday basis. Despite the technological progress, the inhabitants of the world struggle to survive while the surrounding soctiotechnical system renders them powerless—left with the only option to hack the technology to redeem some form of autonomy.

This techno-deterministic nightmare represents the structure of the feeling of the 1980s. It is the feeling of losing oneself in an ever-faster pace of technological progress, mixed with the paradigm of a neoliberal economy and the false promises of free markets postulated by politicians like Margret Thatcher and Ronald

---

skirted the most obvious traps, and mapped the route he'd take through Sense/Net's ice. It was good ice. Wonderful ice. … Its rainbow pixel maze was the first thing he saw when he woke. He'd go straight to the deck, not bothering to dress, and jack in. He was cutting it. He was working. He lost track of days." (Gibson 2016, p. 67).

[6]The pages referenced are from the 2016 version of Neuromancer published with Gollancz.

[7]Cyberpunk emerged in the 1980s around authors like Lewis Shiner, Rudy Rucker, John Shirley, Bruce Sterling and William Gibson. The term itself stems from Bruce Bethke's short story "Cyberpunk" (1983) and was used by Dozois, a science fiction publisher, to describe this collection of young authors. The label was highly controversial, as Suvin says: "Perhaps it might be more useful to say that there is the writer William Gibson, and then there are a couple of expert PR men (most prominently Sterling himself) who know full well the commercial value of an instantly recognizable label." (Suvin 1991, p. 365).

Reagan. Within this breeding ground, Cyberpunk quickly transcended the boundaries of fiction. The media artifacts like films,[8] mangas[9] and video games,[10] which defined the aesthetic and narrative tropes of the genre, gave technophiles an inspiring set of myths to identify with:

> "The Cyberpunks presented themselves as 'techno-urban-guerrilla' artists announcing that both the technological dreams and nightmares envisioned by previous generations of SF artists were already in place, and that writers as well as the general public needed to create ways of using this technology for our own purposes before we all became mere software, easy deletable from the hard drives of multinationalism's vast mainframe." (McCaffery 1991, p. 12)

Cyberpunk was written at a time when the actual possibilities of these new technologies were not yet foreseeable, let alone a statement about their social embedding could be made. The technological futures represented in the genre were mere images of the futures as the future itself. Nonetheless, those fictional images influenced other discourses as well and went far beyond the SF-literature. As Gibson himself points out in an interview:

> "At a certain point I saw cyberpunk jump from being a literary description to being a description of something in the real world. I think the New York Times used it in a headline. 'Last year cyberpunks do something' and I said, You know, I thought they were referring to this group of writers I'm associated with, but in fact, they were referring to outlaw hacker sewer." (Trench 1990, p. 4:57)

With his novel, Gibson was not only re-creating the pessimistic, social and sociotechnical imaginaries of his generation, but also distributing them into different contexts through the neologisms he coined. The most influential one is Gibson's term *Cyberspace*. It became a popular metaphor and created a common understanding of something not yet existing. By that, it facilitated the communication between the public and science, between research and industry or even assisted with the procurement of funds for research projects (Schröter 2004, p. 32).

---

[8]The first era started with "Blade Runner" (Scott 1982) and ended with "The Matrix" (Wachowskis 1999), which was the official moment where the movement became mainstream. In literature, this moment was reached with Stephenson's ironic approach to the genre in his novel "Snow Crash" (Stephenson 1992). Afterwards the second era, called *post*-cyberpunk (Kelly and Kessel 2007b), began and created a vast number of different x-punk derivates (e.g. Steampunk, Biopunk, and others).

[9]Prominent examples from Japan are "Akira" (Ôtomo 1988) and "Kôkaku Kidôtai" (Oshii 1995), translated as "Ghost in the Shell", to name but a few.

[10]As for example the "Metaru Gia"-series by Hideo Kojima, first release in 1987.

In this understanding, Gibson's *Neuromancer* was not only a pioneering work for an innovative literary genre but it also shaped the way people outside of literature thought about digital media. Gibson created a culturally shared image of a future, which everyone was able to reference to when talking about digital technologies. However, the underlying connotation was a grime and dystopic vision of a society determined and changed by those new technologies.

This essay will analyze the storyworld of *Neuromancer* and trace the assumptions about the sociotechnical changes. For the beginning I will (1) explain the concept of *sociotechnical Imaginaries* by Jasanoff and Kim (2015), which stands for the culturally shared visions and potential social changes achieved through new technologies. This perspective guides my analysis and connects to the narratological discussions about (2) the *storyworld*, the description of the social and physical reality of the novel's protagonists. In non-mimetic literature, like SF, special attention is given to the storyworld as the practice of building a deviant world is seen as a unique form of art. Both concepts, sociotechnical imaginaries and storyworlds, show interesting parallels as they deal with the assumptions of how new technologies might define an imaginary society. Afterwards I will (3) examine the storyworld of *Neuromancer* to describe how Gibson anticipated the way that digital technologies redistribute social power.

2 Sociotechnical Imaginaries

In recent years the term *Imaginaries* became common in anthropology and cultural studies to describe terms like *culture* or *cultural beliefs*.[11] Taylor for example defined the concept of *social* imaginaries as "the way we imagine our society" (Taylor 2003, p. 92) and refers to the assumptions used by ordinary people[12] to imagine social life, the social fabrication of power as well as how the society is (or ought to be) structured:

> "By social imaginary, I mean something much broader and deeper than the intellectual schemes people may entertain when they think about social reality in a disengaged mode. I am thinking, rather, of the ways people imagine their social existence, how they fit together with others, how things go on between them and their fellows, the

---

[11] For a comprehensive overview of the term see Strauss (2006) or Gatens (2020).

[12] Strauss (2006) says: "This means talking, not about 'the imaginary of a society', but of people's imaginaries. This person-centered approach recognizes the importance of learned cultural understandings but does not take 'culture' to be a fixe entity assumed to be held in common by a geographically bounded or self-identified group" (Strauss 2006, p. 323).

expectations that are normally met, and the deeper normative notions and images that underlie these expectations." (ibid., p. 23)

Social imaginaries thus define the background understanding of a social group. They are based upon a shared understanding and imply "how we stand to each other, how we got where we are, how we relate to other groups and so on." (ibid., p. 25) Social groups, as understood here, can range from smaller collectives (e.g. families, subcultures, companies, etc.) to larger societies (e.g. nation states, religious collectives, etc.). According to Taylor, imaginaries usually start as theories hold by a few and later—if successful—become social imaginaries through social diffusion within the group. They are produced and reproduced through a repertoire of culturally known practices, images, stories, myths, and legends, which are shared among the members of the group.

Jasanoff and Kim build upon the concept of social imaginaries to close the gap between cultural theory and the study of science and technology (STS). Their concept of sociotechnical imaginaries describes the shared assumptions, hopes and fears regarding the social impact of new and emerging tech (NEST):

"Sociotechnical imaginaries are 'collectively held and performed visions of desirable futures' (or of resistance against the undesirable) ... 'animated by shared understandings of forms of social life and social order attainable through', and supportive of, advances in science and technology." (Jasanoff 2015a, p. 19)

While the concept of sociotechnical imaginaries is referring to NEST, meaning technologies that are not socially embedded yet but still in research or development (Grunwald 2018), Jasanoff and Kim (2015) shift the temporal perspective from Taylors focus on how the present is imagined to how social groups imagine to change/be changed through new technologies in the future. Imagined, because with new and emerging technologies, there is no empirical evidence of their future impact on society which renders all assumptions as imaginations.[13]

It should be stressed that the concept of sociotechnical imaginaries goes beyond encoding visions of what NEST might be capable of but rather what underlying values define how life ought, or ought not, to be lived, as they express

---

[13]This also connects to the differentiation between "present futures" and "future presents" (Luhmann 1990). "Future presents" describes a specific state of affairs later than now, which for obvious reasons does not offer any empirical data to observe. On the other hand, "present futures" refers to *current* images of the future, which are part of the *current* social reality and by that can be observed in discourses and actions already in the present. This sociological turn towards future (in future studies also known as *critical* future studies) therefore shifts the focus from "*Looking into* the future" to "*Looking at* the future" (Brown, et al. 2000).

a shared understanding of social values and what is perceived as good or evil (Jasanoff 2015a, p. 4). In other words, sociotechnical imaginaries "build on the world as it is, but they also project futures as they ought [or ought not] to be." (Jasanoff 2015b, p. 323).

Although most of the work done in the field is focusing on the actual discourse surrounding different NESTs (often in a technopolitical context), it is widely acknowledge that SF—despite its fictional character—has an destinct impact on reality. As Jasanoff says: "Science Fiction is a repository of sociotechnical imaginaries, visions that integrate futures of growing knowledge and technological mastery with normative assessments of what such futures could and should mean for present-day societies." (ibid., p. 337) Therefore, their theoretical concept offers an interesting approach not only for political or cultural theory but for scholars from the field of media studies as well—especially for SF-studies.

By analyzing SF narrations, we can uncover the sociotechnical imaginaries guiding the anticipatory extrapolation of the author, as the ideas and assumptions presented in the story are not presenting a future present but instead represent the imaginaries of the author's *zero world*,[14] the foundation on which his/her speculation is based upon—or as Eshun says: "Looking back at the genre, it becomes apparent that science fiction was never concerned with the future, but rather with engineering feedback between its preferred future and its becoming present." (Eshun 2003, p. 290).

The question remains, how can we uncover the imaginaries inscribed within the worlds of SF narrations? With regards to a methodological approach Jasanoff (2015a, p. 24) says:

> "The methods best suited to studying sociotechnical imaginaries (…) are the methods of interpretive research and analysis that probe the nature of structure—agency relationships through inquiries into meaning making. Although few of these methods are specific to the analysis of sociotechnical imaginaries, they can be applied in ways that are especially attuned to this concept: by attending to the means by which imaginaries frame and represent alternative futures, link past and future times, enable or restrict actions in space, and naturalize ways of thinking about possible worlds."

To trace the sociotechnical imaginary, on which SF-narrations are based, I propose to focus on the architecture of the storyworld, as the imaginaries and the values implied are made explicit In the storyworlds of SF (Fischer and Mehnert 2020).

---

[14]Zero world meaning the contemporary context of the author at the time he/she wrote the story. Or as Suvin puts it: the "empirically verifiable properties around the author." (Suvin 1972, p. 377).

Analyzing the elements and the dynamic interplay between the elements of this possible world allows probing the structure—agency relationship. This can be done through an approach called *Critical Worldbuilding* (Ekman and Taylor 2016), which I will explain below.

3 Storyworlds and Worldbuilding

> "All right. There's a text in front of you. For over determined reasons [we] know it's SF ... The moment we recognize the situation [in the story] as non normal ..., certain questions that are associated with SF come into play: 'What in the world portrayed by the story is responsible for the transformation?' ... What in the portrayed world of the story, by statement or by implication, must be different from ours in order for this sentence to be normally uttered? (That is, how does the condition of possibility in the world of the story differ from ours?) But whether the text satisfies or subverts these expectations, the reading experience is still controlled by them." (Delany 1987)

As SF author Delany points out, Science Fiction strongly builds upon an estranged experience of a world different to the world of the reader. While reading the story, the recipient is steadily trying to reorient and understand the inherent logic of the world of the story. This so-called storyworld is hidden behind the protagonist's dilemmas, the plot structure and the specific conflicts of a story. It constitutes and holds the narration while creating the mundane everyday situations that all fictional characters encounter as the story unfolds.

Therefore, the storyworld of a story expands beyond the story itself. This means, a storyworld can host multiple stories simultaneously, extend across various media or even exist without a story at all but instead appear in different forms such as "appendices, maps, timelines, glossaries of invented languages, and so forth." (Wolf 2012, p. 2).[15]

---

[15] The term Transmedia Storytelling (Jenkins 2007) describes how the story world extends beyond a single story and spreads across different media formats. It also crosses the area between the fictional and the real. In reference to Stuart Hall, Jenkins points out that pop culture has power, i.e. it creates a public sphere of imagination from which actors can draw new narratives to feedback into the discourse. This happens not only in the NEST discourses, but also in socio-political struggles of minorities who want to define their status in a society (see Jenkins 2020). The recent examples of women marching in costumes from the Storyworld of Atwood's "Handmaid's Tale" (1985) are illustrating this case.

Deconstructing Cyberpunk Worlds

Despite the more than 200 years long history of the SF-genre, the theoretical focus on understanding and analyzing storyworlds and the process of worldbuilding[16] has been introduced to narratology fairly recent.[17]

To understand the concept of the storyworld, Wolf builds upon the differentiation done by Tolkien between the *Primary World*, the actual world in which we live, and the *Secondary World*, the imaginary world created by an author (Wolf 2012, p. 23). The relationship between both worlds goes beyond the dichotomy of *fictional* and *real* but instead is structured (a) hierarchically, as the Primary World contains Secondary Worlds, and (b) by a degree of deviation called *secondariness*, which is "varying with the strength of the connection to the Primary World." (ibid., p. 25) The secondariness of an imagined world is defined by the *Novum*, the fictitious novelty(ies) of every SF-story (Suvin 1979, p. 94). The Novum can exist in different orders of magnitude and range from single (or several) deviations to whole milieus and changing environments. Most prominent in the genre, especially in Near-Future Science-Fiction, is the use of new technologies (Mehnert 2019).[18] However, the Novum can be every element within the world like a social or political change,[19] environmental change[20] or other external or internal forces affecting society—or even everything at once as done in Cyberpunk:

"Cyberpunk realized that the old SF structure of 'alter only one thing and see what happens' was hopelessly outdated, a doctrine rendered irrelevant by the furious pace of late 20th century technological change. The future isn't 'just one damn thing after another,' it's every damn thing all at the same time." (Person 1998)

This being said, the term *World*, as used in this context, does not only refer to geographical or spatial categories but is used in an experiential sense which covers "everything that is experienced by the characters." (Wolf 2012, p. 25).

Storyworlds, although being fictional, exist in the Primary World, as we can refer to them, talk about them but also experience them by immersing into stories presented through books, films, video games and other media formats that contain texts.[21] Ryan (2001, p. 91) says:

---

[16] Understood here as the deliberate process of creating a storyworld.
[17] Most prominently by Ryan (1991), Dolezel (2000), Herman (2004) and Wolf (2012).
[18] as in Minority Report (Spielberg 2002) where the Novum *Precrime* changed the architecture of the city (von Stackelberg and McDowell 2015, p. 37).
[19] as in Atwoods "The Handmaid's Tale" (Atwood 1985).
[20] as in climate fiction like "New York 2140" (Robinson 2018).
[21] *Text* is here understood beyond literature but rather as the content of media.

"The text is apprehended as a window on something that exists outside language and extends in time and space well beyond the window frame. To speak of a textual world means to draw a distinction between a realm of language, made of names, definite descriptions, sentences, and propositions, and an extralinguistic realm of characters, objects, facts, and states of affairs serving as referents to the linguistic expressions."

Understanding narrative texts as windows into other worlds means to rely on the linguistic expressions, which allow access to the realm of the extralinguistic, the world behind the text. This demands a specific reading of a story. Generally speaking: A compelling story and a compelling world are two different things. While it is usually the plot-driven parts that draw the reader into the world, it is the descriptive passages that slow down the plot to give a depth understanding of the world surrounding the character. It is these descriptive passages that are at the center of analyses of storyworlds.

4 Critical Worldbuilding in *Neuromancer*

One of the reasons for the uniqueness of Gibson's writing is the way he introduces the reader to the storyworld.[22] In his novels, he describes the setting in meticulous details with a dizzyingly amount of information, while at the same time, he does seldom explain the elements or the connections of the elements between each other or towards the Primary World of the reader.[23] This way, he is creating a "sensory overload that submerges the reader in the literary equivalent of the hard-rock 'wall of sound'" (Sterling 1986, p. xv). The following quote gives an example:

> "Case ... turned and walked past a vast, brilliantly lit newsstand, the covers of dozens of glossy Japanese magazines presenting the faces of the month's newest simstim stars. Directly overhead, along the nighted axis, the hologram sky glittered with fanciful

---

[22]There are different forms of worldbuilding, which I will explain in the following footnotes. The *authorial* worldbuilding defines the sequential, iterative, and segmental process of creating a storyworld through adding, changing, or developing elements in a storyworld (Ekman and Taylor 2016, p. 10).

[23]A typical moment in SF is the connection to the Primary world. For example in form of a chronic or a historian, usually and old man, reminiscing of the past (the present of the reader) and explaining how the world has become the world we see. For example, in the movie Matrix (Wachowskis 1999) this is done by Morpheus, in Soylent Green (Fleischer 1973) it is the character Sol Roth who tells the audience how their world became his world. In Neuromancer, Gibson is not using those elements at all but leaving out almost anything that offers orientation.

constellations suggesting playing cards, the faces of dice, a top hat, a martini glass." (Gibson 2016, p. 165)

In this quote, Gibson refers to *Simstim Stars* but does not bother to explain it. Instead, it becomes a mundane element in the storyworld, which—by not explaining it—appears to be even more mundane.

The *Simstim* technology, which has been introduced earlier in the novel, is an augmentation of the physical sensorium. It allows its users to experience the sensory stimulation of another person. Within the story, we see how Case uses it to *flip in* to the sensorium of a second character, called Molly, and to feel what she feels:

"'How you doing, Case?' He heard the words and felt her form them. She slid a hand into her jacket, a fingertip circling a nipple under warm silk. The sensation made him catch his breath. She laughed. But the link was one-way. He had no way to reply." (ibid., p. 63)

Although Gibson explains the technology *Simstim*, the concept of Simstim *Stars* is not explained and only referred to twice in the whole novel. In another part, the reader gets introduced to one of these stars, a celebrity called *Tally Isham*—again, just as a sidenote:

"Cowboys didn't get into Simstim, he [Case] thought, because it was basically a meat toy. He knew that the trodes he used and the little plastic tiara dangling from a Simstim deck were basically the same, and that the cyberspace matrix was actually a drastic simplification of the human sensorium, at least in terms of presentation, but Simstim itself struck him as a gratuitous multiplication of flesh input. The commercial stuff was edited, of course, so that if Tally Isham got a headache in the course of a segment, you didn't feel it." (ibid., p. 62)

Gibson is hinting at the usage of *Simstim* for "commercial stuff", but leaves it at a hint. From here on, it is left to the reader to speculate about a possible economic infrastructure evolving around the technological Novum,[24] as the description of the world does not offer any more details about the new media ecology. It becomes obvious, that an author cannot explain all aspects of a Secondary World. Dolezel emphasizes that "it would take a text of infinite length to construct a complete

---

[24]This is what Ekman and Taylor call "the *readerly* worldbuilding" (2016, p. 10). It describes the construction of a mental model of the world in the mind of the reader during the reception of the story. See also Herman's concept of "cognitive narratology." (Herman 2013).

fictional world" (Dolezel 2000, p. 169). Therefore, incompleteness is a necessary property of Secondary Worlds.

This becomes important when critically examining a storyworld. Instead of focusing on the creative process of the author or the reception of the reader, a *critical* worldbuilding approach solely focuses on the information given by the text and does not extrapolate it or develop the world by logical implications. Instead part of the analyses is the way in which world elements are presented, their context and various relations, and their meaning from a theoretical viewpoint (Ekman and Taylor 2016, p. 11). Therefore, an important part of critical worldbuilding is the close reading of elements in the world and what details can be inferred and deduced that construct the world around them (Taylor and Ekman 2019, p. 22).

The critical reflection of a storyworld further allows to uncover the implicit narratives entangled within the novel. To reconnect this to the bigger picture mentioned in the beginning, this endeavor is not to be understood as a mere text or literature analysis. Instead, the interwoven narratives used in *Neuromancer* are a representation of the contemporary sociotechnical imaginaries of the 1980s.

Therefore, the critical worldbuilding approach becomes a starting point to trace the author's implicit imaginaries of "forms of social life and social order attainable through, and supportive of, advances in science and technology" (Jasanoff 2015a, p. 19), which are to be understood as representational for a whole generation.

Furthermore, those narratives find their way from the fictional world of *Neuromancer* into the non-fictional world or reality, as they connect to the metaphors used in the subsequent discourses about new and emerging technologies. By that they shape the abstract sociotechnical imaginaries and the concrete images surrounding digital media technologies which influence the visions of NEST (Grunwald 2018), the technopolitical decision-making processes that lead into the funding of those developments (Schröter 2004; Jasanoff 2015a), and last but not least the actual development itself as it opens up a space of potentialities (Waffender 1991).

In the following chapter, I will analyze the storyworld of William Gibson's novel *Neuromancer* (1984) with a particular focus on how digital media is embedded within the storyworld, how it redefines the power structures within the world and on the (sociotechnical) ecosystem around *Cyberspace*—or as Gibson introduces it: "the consensual hallucination that was the matrix." (ibid., p. 6).

5 The Different Worlds of the *Neuromancer* Novel

For a better understanding of how the described sociotechnical imaginary is woven into the imaginary world, I will structure the analysis in three chapters that go along the three connected worlds of the novel[25]:

1. The Primary World is here defined as the world in which the author William Gibson exists (also known as the Zero World of the author). Here I will reflect on the socio-political context from which Gibson starts his extrapolation.
2. I'll enter the Secondary World through the Neuromancer novel.[26] The novel reveals the world of the protagonist Case, which has some similarities to the Primary World, as some places have the same name (e.g. Tokyo, Istanbul, Chiba or Boston). However, the world is inhabited by different characters and is technologically estranged.
3. The third layer, which lays within this strangely familiar but alienated world, is called *Cyberspace matrix*, a spatial and visual representation of data from different computers. It is a dreamlike world within the Secondary World—a landscape simulation. Case enters the *Cyberspace* through a digital medium—a hacked device known as *Ono-Sendai Cyberspace 7* or simply *deck*.

5.1 Gibson's World

"We believed that science fiction needed to take its cues from the present—computer technology, corporate power structures, Japanese economic ascendency—rather than the mid-century pipe dreams of World Governments and Galactic Federations. For

---

[25] "A first step in a critical world-building venture could be to determine how many fictional worlds are actually present, and how they relate to each other." (Taylor and Ekman 2019, p. 21).

[26] Gibson himself created several entry points into the Neuromancer-Universe: the three novels Neuromancer (1984), Count Zero (1986) and Mona Lisa Overdrive (1988). Additionally, there are three short stories that play in the same world: Johnny Mnemonic (1981), Burning Chrome (1982), and New Rose Hotel (1984). All published in the Sci-Fi magazine Omni. Beyond his own publications there is a graphic novel adaptation of Neuromancer (Haven and Jensen 1989), the Neuromancer Video game (1988), a comprehensive wiki-page on fandom.com created by fans of the universe (William Gibson Wiki—Sprawl trilogy) and several more media artifacts. However, as Gibson is the only author of this world, only the contributions coming from him are counting as canon. He alone already created an extremely dense and detailed world with a huge amount of elements to focus on and to write about. For the sake of this paper, I will mainly focus on the descriptions given in Neuromancer.

me, the movement was about global culture, anarchy and high-energy prose." (Shiner 1991)

To understand the Neuromancer world, it's important to understand the zero world of the author—meaning the major changes in the '80s that gave birth to the genre of Cyberpunk. For one, this was the production of high-tech for the consumer market. In the 1980s, Technology became smaller and more manageable, it became a consumer friendly commodity and through the market an ordinary part of everyday life: "Tech sticks to the skin, responds to the touch: the personal computer, the Sony Walkman, the portable telephone, the soft contact lens." (Sterling 1986, p. xiii) Technology was not secretly created behind locked doors or in concealed laboratories, developed by expert geniuses or evil doctors, as depicted in SF before. Instead the cyberpunk authors grew up in a surrounding where new media gadgets became affordable and mundane, as McCaffery points out: "The cyberpunks were the first generation of artists for whom the technologies of satellite dishes, video and audio players and recorders, computer and video games (both of particular importance), digital watches, and MTV were not exoticisms, but part of a daily 'reality matrix'" (McCaffery 1991, p. 12).

The second change took place on a geopolitical level and led to a new economic order. New markets opened up worldwide, multi- and transnational organizations were founded—often in the field of digital technology—and globalization was driven by the neo-liberal agenda of politicians from the USA and Europe. In the 1980s, Western societies entered an era that can best be described by what Jameson calls "late capitalism" (1991, p. xviii):

> "Besides the forms of transnational business mentioned above, [Late Capitalisms] features include the new international division of labor, a vertiginous new dynamic in international banking and the stock exchanges (including the enormous Second and Third World debt), new forms of media interrelationship (very much including transportation systems such as containerization), computers and automation, the flight of production to advanced Third World areas, along with all the more familiar social consequences, including the crisis of traditional labor, the emergence of yuppies, and gentrification on a now-global scale."

Companies acting within this globe-spanning system are dependent upon rapid innovation and technological progress for their own advancements while competing with other companies for further expansion. As competition builds upon highly specialized marketing information, the development of digital technology for collecting data to create and organize information, became their key priority: "The key 'global resource' is the *information itself* rather that the oil, farm good, or other resources usually associated with capitalist market systems." (McCaffery 1991, p. 4) Such developments have created an expansion of the realm of multinationals in which the "'dance of biz' can whirl free and infiltrate the desires of the soul." (Gibson quoted in McCaffery 1991, p. 5).

Both developments are at the core of the cyberpunk worlds, as Jameson says, they have "crystallized in a new type of science fiction, called cyberpunk, which is fully as much an expression of transnational corporate realities as it is of global paranoia itself" (Jameson 1991, p. 38). Jameson therefore calls Cyberpunk "the supreme literary expression if not of postmodernism, then of late capitalism itself" (1991, p. 419).

In Neuromancer, the economical changes appear in form of the *Zaibatsus*, that gained control over the society, while the technological innovations come closer to the body, penetrate it or merge with the mind, and create new forms of control and power while cutting down the agency of its users.

5.2 The Neuromancer World

> "Power, in Case's world, meant corporate power. The Zaibatsus, the multinationals that shaped the course of human history, had transcended old barriers. Viewed as organisms, they had attained a kind of immortality." (Gibson 2016, p. 224)

Gibson's vision of an extrapolated late-capitalistic society is manifested in the concept of the *Zaibatsus*,[27] powerful multinational corporations that control whole economies (see also "Zaibatsu"). The largest *Zaibatsu* in the *Neuromancer* world is *Hosaka*, a computer company that produced the *deck* Case uses to enter the *Cyberspace*. Similar to the reflection on the *simstim stars*, his descriptions are rather thin and appear as side notes. At one point Case mentions that *Zaibatsu* employees are "working all [their] life for one zaibatsu. Company housing, company hymn, company funeral" (Gibson 2016, p. 43). Schmeink states that a Zaibatsu "extends its rigorous hold on people beyond even their life." (2015, p. 225) Therefore, the multinationals become a metaphor for capitalism and how it is imagined to pervade the life of the inhabitants of the fictional world.[28]

---

[27]We see examples in other Cyberpunk universes as well, like Weyland-Yutani in the Alien universe, Skynet in the Terminator-franchise or the Tyrell Cooperation from Blade Runner.

[28]This is one of the major tropes in Cyberpunk: "Cyberpunk worlds are not set in some far distant but in a near future world, in which technology and hypercapitalism have become dominant and the urban landscape has increasingly usurped nature. The worlds of cyberpunk deal with mega-corporations, which rule the planet, with a fierce form of capitalism and an

The Neuromancer world in general is a dystopia where the *Zaibatsus* are one example for the major theme of the novel: Powerlessness.

Dolezel writes, that power "is perhaps the strongest motivational factor" (Dolezel 2000, p. 106) for characters within fictional worlds. Within the Neuromancer world, power is not only exercised by other actors directly but also through digital technologies, which leaves the characters within the dystopian world powerless. In the following I will give three examples:

1. The *Cut-Out Chip*.
2. The *Construct*.
3. *Cyberspace* and the ability to *Cut Off*.

5.2.1 The *Cut-Out Chip* and *Molly Millions*

Digital technology presented in the Secondary World is directly linked to the brain, either through neuronal implants or through external sensor stimulation. This allows to separate the mind from the body to either create a body without a mind or to create a mind without a body.

The former is explained in the backstory of Molly. A female character who is introduced as a tough mercenary in her first dialogue with Case:

> "My name's Molly. I'm collecting you for the man I work for. Just wants to talk, is all. Nobody wants to hurt you ... 'Cept I do hurt people sometimes, Case. I guess it's just the way I'm wired." (Gibson 2016, p. 29)

Molly's body is augmented by several implants such as mirror-shaded glasses that have been surgically inserted in front of her eyes, blades that slide out and retract beneath her fingernails, and a *neural cut out chip*, which she used in her former life as a *meat puppet*[29] working in a *puppet parlor*[30]:

> "Once they plant the cut-out chip, it seems like free money. Wake up sore, sometimes, but that's it. Renting the goods, is all. You aren't in, when it's all happening." (Gibson 2016, p. 162)

---

increasing shear between rich and poor, leaving most of humanity down and out." (Schmeink 2015, p. 222).

[29] *Meat puppets* are sex workers without their conscious mind.

[30] According to the Neuromancer fandom glossary, a *pupper parlor* is "a brothel where people loan out their bodies while maintained in a blanked-out state" (see "Molly Millions").

While the mind is *cut out* of the body, the owner of the brothel loads a different mind—in form of *software*—into the body. Molly continues and explains:

> "So the bastard who ran the place, he had some custom software cooked up. Berlin, that's the place for snuff, you know? Big market for mean kicks, Berlin. I never knew who wrote the program they switched me to, but it was based on all the classics. ... And they didn't tell me. They switched the software and started renting to specialty markets." (Gibson 2016, p. 162)

In this example of the use of a *cut-out* chip, Schmeink points out that "the female body becomes a canvas for the virtual sexual desires of its male customers." (Schmeink 2015, p. 227) It is one of the few examples of the use of such a device[31] that is given in the Neuromancer novel. However, based on that example, we can assume that the main usage of the technology is for gaining power over people and rendering the subjects to powerless objects without free will.

5.2.2 The *Construct* Dixie Flatline

The second example is the character *Dixie Flatline*, a human mind that was transformed into a digital computer program. Dixie was a former hacker called *McCoy Pauley* who used to be a mentor of Case. Before he died of a heart attack, he sold a copy of his mind to a *Zaibatsu* called *Sense/Net*—his personality became a *firmware construct* which is saved on a *ROM cassette*. *Constructs* are digital copies of a persons "memory/personality, replicating his memories, skills, obsessions, even kneejerk responses" (see also "Construct"). In the novel, Case hacks into *Sense/Net* to steal the *ROM* that contains Dixie, as he needs his help to hack into more complicated systems in the continuous plot.

Although Dixie is technically immortal, his existence became merely a simulacrum of his actual life as he "does not live in any human sense of the word." (Schmeink 2015, p. 229) When Case asks Dixie, whether he is sentient or not, his answer is: "Well, it feels like I am, kid, but I'm really just a bunch of ROM. It's one of them, ah, philosophical questions, I guess ..." (Gibson 2016, p. 85). Dixie follows the archetype of the Genie in a bottle, whose only existence is to serve his master—which is Case. His own wishes are described at the end the following conversation. Dixie asks Case:

> "'Do me a favor, boy.'

---

[31] The other one is a short passage a few lines before within the same context: "The girl sat up in bed and said something in German. Her eyes were soft and unblinking. Automatic pilot. A neural cut-out." (Gibson 2016, p. 161).

'What's that, Dix?'
'This scam of yours, when it's over, you erase this goddam thing.'" (ibid., p. 118)

With "Scam of yours", Dixie refers to his own existence as a construct. His only wish is to be deleted as he cannot continue this existence nor commit suicide himself. Dixie's whole existent is reduced to the capability of the ROM. His mind lives in the *Cyberspace*, his main interactions are with Case inside of the *Cyberspace* where he is following Cases order and supporting him on his quest. His free will and whole existence is reduced to the efficiency of his tasks to support Case. As Dixie is the only *Construct* we get introduced to in the *Neuromancer* novel, it's not possible to reflect upon other examples. However, the digital technology of the *Construct* is again a new technology of control, as the *Constructs* itself are totally reliant on the usage of their owner. Although Case and Dixie get along and build a friendship over the course of the story, Case is still the power holder while Dixie becomes the subordinate agent, which is not due to his free decision but instead due to the technology involved.

5.3 The Cyberspace

"In Neuromancer, one form of technology—cyberspace—stands as a gateway to a universe of visionary intensity. At the same time, it is also a tool used to control information and people" (Olsen 1992, p. 71)

In the storyworld of *Neuromancer*, digital technology is not only used to separate the body from the mind but also as an access point into the world of *Cyberspace*, a spatial representation of data and a world within the Secondary World of the novel. *Cyberspace* has its roots in "primitive arcade games, ... early graphics programs and military experimentation with cranial jacks" (Gibson 2016, p. 59).

The technology to enter *Cyberspace* comes in form of a *deck*, the *Ono-Sendai Cyberspace 7*, and its peripheral connectors, which are called *dermatrodes* or *trodes*. The *trodes* are sense stimulators, attached to a "black terry sweat-band across [the] forehead" (ibid., p. 59) of the user. The *trodes* stimulate the brain and transport the "disembodied consciousness into the consensual hallucination that was the matrix" (ibid., p. 6), a process called *jacking in*. It allows the mind to transcend the body while the body is left unconscious—even up to the point of a braindeath, where the body looses it's vital functions. This process is known as *flatlining*—"the man was dead, flat down braindeath." (ibid., p. 87).

The first time Case *jacks in* to *Cyberspace* is depicted as follows:

"Disk beginning to rotate, faster, becoming a sphere of paler gray. Expanding—And flowed, flowered for him, fluid neon origami trick, the unfolding of his distance less home, his country, transparent 3D chessboard extending to infinity. Inner eye opening to the stepped scarlet pyramid of the Eastern Seaboard Fission Authority burning beyond the green cubes of Mitsubishi Bank of America, and high and very far away he saw the spiral arms of military systems, forever beyond his reach." (ibid., p. 60)

The *Cyberspace* is as a landscape simulation (Suvin 1991, p. 355) which consists of different forms of content. On one hand, it is occupied by a spatial representation of the world where *Zaibatsus* and other institutions hold a digital copy of their spatial equivalent. It appears as a parallel universe of Case's actual world: "When Case jacked in, he opened his eyes to the familiar configuration of the Eastern Seaboard Fission Authority's Aztec pyramid of data." (Gibson 2016, p. 118) In the virtual realm, the multinationals are represented in form of pyramid headquarters. However, in this world it is Case who is able to *hack through the ICE* to gain access to the pyramids and steal the data of the *Zaibatsus*—it is Case who has power over them in *Cyberspace*. This is the moment of empowerment for the low-life *console cowboys* in the *Neuromancer* world, as "they (and only they— not the rulers obscenely devoted to money or power) are capable of [hacking]" (Suvin 1991, p. 356). Seen from this perspective, *Cyberspace* becomes a refugee for Case, which is also the reason why he is suffering under the loss of his ability to *jack in* at the beginning of the novel.

On the other hand the *Cyberspace* can become a deceptive simulation of the reality that feels just like Case's real world, as, despite the physical separation of body and mind, *Cyberspace* builds up on strong bodily stimulation, as the following situation out of the virtual world describes:

"A wind was rising. Sand stung his cheek. He put his face against his knees and wept, the sound of his sobbing as distant and alien as the cry of the searching gull. Hot urine soaked his jeans, dribbled on the sand, and quickly cooled in the wind off the water. When his tears were gone, his throat ached. … He shivered, it was with a cold that finally forced him to stand. His knees and elbows ached. His nose was running; he wiped it on the cuff of his jacket, then searched one empty pocket after another. 'Jesus,' he said, shoulders hunched, tucking his fingers beneath his arms for warmth. 'Jesus.' His teeth began to chatter." (ibid., p. 258)

In the quoted situation, Case is *cut off* by an artificial intelligence called *Neuromancer*, the alleged antagonist of the book. To be *cut off* means, that the mind of the user is hold captive inside of *Cyberspace*, up to the point that the mindless brain of the user dies and he/she *flatlines*. This is happening twice to Case. Once in the situation mentioned above and a second time with another A.I. called *Wintermute*: "I'm glad I was able to cut you off before you'd managed to jack out" (ibid., p. 132). In both cases his body was flatlined for several seconds:

"'Mon,' Maelcum was saying, 'I don't like this ...'

'It's cool,' Molly said. 'It's just okay. It's something these guys do, is all. Like, he wasn't dead, and it was only a few seconds ...'

'I saw th' screen, EEG readin' dead. Nothin' movin', forty second.'

'Well, he's okay now.'

'EEG flat as a strap,' Maelcum protested." (ibid., p. 134)

One could argue for the utopian potential of cyberspace, as it enables the overcoming of the dualism of body and mind and could thus solve questions of gender prejudice or racism. Instead, Gibson again plays with the narrative of powerlessness when describing technology. "This time it is the technology itself that becomes the autonomous power owner as the human becomes the subordinate actor. In the example of *Cyberspace*, it is an artificial intelligence that gains control over a person's consciousness by cutting Case off from its own body."

6 Re-Imagining Cyberpunk? The Anti-Dystopian Solar Sunrise

"What Science Fiction is about it's not literal prediction of what will happen fifty years from now or five thousands years from now. It's an examination of certain potentials that exist in our situation. It's a fiction but it's a fiction about things, which really exist in our present. But they exist in the mode of potentiality rather than in the mode of what's physically, actually here." (Shaviro quoted in Roth 2015, p. 53:58)

Gibson's debut novel became an important milestone in SF literature. In addition to its great influence on the genre, it also captured the prevailing preoccupation of his generation with the possible changes brought about by technological progress and neoliberalism. The synthesis is a dystopian world where the inhabitants are powerless in the face of digital technologies such as artificial intelligence, virtual reality and a digital network. It becomes a snapshot in time and presents, what Shaviro calls, the "mode of potentiality" of those technologies.

As the analyses showed, the prevailing imaginary on which the storyworld of *Neuromancer* is built is power- and hopelessness. The characters have no agency but are condemned to live in complex power struggles that are created through digital media: "They lack genuine free will [...] the immachinated individual in Gibson's world does not govern him or herself." (Olsen 1992, p. 71 quoted in Schmeink 2015, p. 230) They become the victims of a life-negating system. This feeling of losing control and subordination towards the technological progress is found in multiple other SF examples following cyberpunk across the globe.

There is an obvious need for dystopian fiction in society. Dystopias uncover possible social developments by extrapolating current trends. These possible developments need to be explored so that we as a society can identify them when they occur and have narratives to ward them off. Fiction is a proven means to do just that. It also means, however, that dystopia is not a wishful thinking about our future, but rather it points to futures that we should prevent.

As important as it is to have present images of futures that we do not want, it is also important to have collective images of futures we do want. Despite the punk aesthetics and counterculture attitude that Gibson and the cyberpunk movement have created, the movement offers no desirable alternatives. Although the console cowboys hack the multinationals in a guerrilla-like warfare against the system, they do exactly that and only that—they fight AGAINST the system without offering the vision of an alternative. What Gibson shows is not how his protagonists use technology to liberate themselves from the Zaibatus, and thus from capitalism itself, instead he depicts them as caught up in the capitalist realism without a way out. Case is "just another hustler, trying to make it through"—hacking the Cyberspace in the hope to regain autonomy. Or as Suvin describes it: "[Gibson] hates the status quo a bit too readily as inevitable and unchangeable." (Suvin 1991, p. 357).

So towards the end I want to pose the question: How can we re-imagine SF in the aftermath of Cyberpunk? In an opinion piece for the New York times, titled "Confessions of an Ex-Cyberpunk" (1991), the SF-author and former Cyberpunk author Lewis Shiner caught on this lack of anti-dystopian thinking:

> "Today's cyberpunk ... offers power fantasies, the same dead-end thrills we get from video games and blockbuster movies like 'Rambo' and 'Aliens.' It gives Nature up for dead, accepts violence and greed as inevitable and promotes the cult of the loner.
>
> I find myself waiting—maybe in vain—for a new literature of idealism and compassion that is contemporary not only on the technological level but also the emotional. It would show the price that must be paid for solutions to our problems; it would see the computer neither as enemy nor god but as a tool for human purposes. I believe that this—not cyberpunk—is the attitude we need to get us into the 21st century." (Shiner 1991)

What Shiner was waiting for is currently appearing as a silver lining on the horizon. The SF-subgenre of *Solarpunk*[32] follows the premise that SF needs a new approach towards the future. It neglects the technodeterministic visions of the '80s and builds storyworlds in which the technology is used and created by the protagonists, mostly in collectives and with a demand for environmentally friendly solutions. Solarpunk narrations are anti-dystopian inspirations for a sustainable future: "the 'solar' in Solarpunk has come to represent not only the ecological aspect of this budding subgenre, but also the idea of brightness and hope." (Lodi-Ribeiro et al. 2018, p. 2) With this approach to technology, the authors try to create a counter-narrative to Cyberpunk. This is seen as a political act, as the stories itself are not only written and publish to define a new SF-genre but rather to inspire engineers, environmentalists or entrepreneurs to find new sociotechnical imaginaries.

However, despite the positive and hopeful attitude, the genre is still far from creating the cultural impact that Gibson's Cyberspace-visions had on non-fictional discourses as well. The reasons for that are manifold: On the one hand, Solarpunk still lacks a common language and a canonical use of neologisms, which can serve as metaphors in non-fictional discourses. On the other hand, the current media landscape is far from being as monolithically as it was in the 80s. Visions of the future are more dispersed and the digital media landscape supports the separation of the multitude of future-imaginaries into smaller information bubbles. But maybe, it simply needs a new William Gibson, an author who is original and gifted enough to re-imagine the cyberpunk visions of the '80s to create a movement that builds on the hopeful sociotechnical imaginaries that address the challenges of the twenty-first century.

References

Akira. Directed by Katsuhiro Otomo. Japan: Toho, 1988.
Atwood, Margaret. 1985. *The handmaid's tale*. Toronto: McClelland and Stewart.
Bethke, Bruce. 1983. Cyberpunk. *AMAZING Science Fiction Stories*. https://project.cyberpunk.ru/lib/cyberpunk/. Accessed 2 Nov. 2020.
Brown, Nik, B. Rappert, and A. Webster, eds. 2000. *Contested futures: A sociology of prospective techno-science*. Aldershot: Ashgate Publishing Limited.
Construct. n.d. William Gibson Wiki. https://williamgibson.fandom.com/wiki/Construct. Accessed 2 Nov. 2020.

---

[32]For an introduction to the genre see Lodi-Ribeiro et al. (2018), Ulibarri et al. (2018), or Grzyb et al. (2017).

Csicsery-Ronay, Istvan. 1991. Cyberpunk and neuromanticism. In *Storming the reality studio: A casebook of cyberpunk & postmodern science fiction: A casebook of cyberpunk and postmodern science fiction*, ed. Larry McCaffery, 182–193. Durham: Duke University Press.
Delany, Samuel R. 1987. The semiology of silence. *Science Fiction Studies* 14 (2): 134–164.
Dolezel, Lubomír. 2000. *Heterocosmica: Fiction and possible worlds*. Baltimore: The Johns Hopkins University Press.
Ekman, Stefan, and A.I. Taylor. 2016. Notes toward a critical approach to worlds and worldbuilding. *Fafnir – Nordic Journal of Science Fiction and Fantasy Research* 3 (3): 7–18.
Eshun, Kodwo. 2003. Further considerations of afrofuturism. *CR: The New Centennial Review*. https://doi.org/10.1353/ncr.2003.0021.
Fischer, Nele, and W. Mehnert. 2020. Building possible worlds. A speculation based research framework to reflect on images of the future. https://jfsdigital.org/building-possible-worlds-a-speculation-based-framework-to-reflect-on-images-of-the-future/. Accessed 2 Nov. 2020.
Gatens, Moira. 2020. Imaginaries. In *50 Concepts for a critical phenomenology*, ed. Gail Weiss, Ann V. Murphy, and Gayle Salamon, 181–188. Evanston: Northwestern University Press.
Gibson, William. 1982. Burning chrome. *Omni* 7: 72–77.
Gibson, William. 2016. *Neuromancer*. London: Gollancz.
Grunwald, Armin. 2018. *Technology assessment in practice and theory*. London: Routledge.
Grzyb, Liz, and C. Sparks, eds. 2017. *Ecopunk!: Speculative tales of radical futures*. Greenwood: Ticonderoga Publications.
De Haven, Tom, and B. Jensen. 1989. *William Gibson's Neuromancer: The graphic novel— Volume 1*. New York: Epic Graphic Novel.
Herman, David. 2004. *Story logic: Problems and possibilities of narrative*. Lincoln: University of Nebraska Press.
Herman, David. 2013. Cognitive narratology. *The living handbook of narratology*. https://www.lhn.uni-hamburg.de/node/38.html. Accessed 2 Nov. 2020.
Jameson, Fredric. 1991. *Postmodernism: Or, the cultural logic of late capitalism*. London: Duke University Press.
Jasanoff, Sheila. 2015a. Future imperfect: Science, technology, and the imaginations of modernity. In *Dreamscapes of modernity: Sociotechnical imaginaries and the fabrication of power*, ed. S.-H. Kim and S. Jasanoff, 1–33. Chicago: University of Chicago Press.
Jasanoff, Sheila. 2015b. Imagined and invented worlds. In *Dreamscapes of modernity: Sociotechnical imaginaries and the fabrication of power*, ed. S.-H. Kim and S. Jasanoff, 321–341. Chicago: University of Chicago Press.
Jasanoff, Sheila, and Sang-Hyun Kim, ed. 2015. *Dreamscapes of Modernity: Sociotechnical Imaginaries and the Fabrication of Power*. 1 edition. Chicago: University of Chicago Press.
Jenkins, Henry. 2007. Transmedia storytelling. https://henryjenkins.org/2007/03/transmedia_storytelling_101.html. Accessed 2 Nov. 2020.
Jenkins, Henry, G. Peters-Lazaro, and S. Shresthova. 2020. *Popular culture and the civic imagination: Case studies of creative social change*. New York: New York University Press.

Kelly, James Patrick, and J. Kessel. 2007a. Introduction. In *Rewired: The post-cyberpunk anthology*, ed. J.P. Kelly and J. Kessel. San Francisco: Tachyon Publications.
Kelly, James Patrick, and J. Kessel, eds. 2007b. *Rewired: The post-cyberpunk anthology*. San Francisco: Tachyon Publications.
Kôkaku Kidôtai. Directed by Mamoru Oshii. Japan; United Kingdom: Shochiku; Manga Entertainment, 1995.
Lodi-Ribeiro, Gerson, et al. 2018. *Solarpunk: Ecological and fantastical stories in a sustainable world*. Oklahoma: World Weaver Press.
Luhmann, Niklas. 1990. Die Zukunft Kann Nicht Beginnen: Temporalstrukturen Der Modernen Gesellschaft. In *Vor Der Jahrtausendwende: Berichte Zur Lage Der Zukunft 1. + 2. Band, Preis JE Buch*, ed. Peter Sloterdijk. Frankfurt a. M.: Suhrkamp.
McCaffery, Larry. 1991. Introduction: The desert of the real. In *Storming the reality studio: A casebook of cyberpunk & postmodern science fiction: A casebook of cyberpunk and postmodern science fiction*, ed. Larry McCaffery. New Durham: DUKE UNIV PR.
Mehnert, Wenzel. 2019. Dystopische Möglichkeitsräume—Near Future Science Fiction Als Schnittstelle Zu Möglichen Zukünften. In *Unheimliche Schnittstellen / Uncanny Interfaces Textem Verlag Hamburg*, ed. K.D. Haensch, L. Nelke, and M. Planitzer. Hamburg: Textem Verlag.
Molly Millions. n.d. William Gibson Wiki. https://williamgibson.fandom.com/wiki/Molly_Millions. Accessed 11 Mar. 2020.
Olsen, Lance. 1992. *William Gibson: Starmont Reader's Guide, No 58*, 1st ed. San Bernardino: Borgo Press.
Person, Lawrence. 1998. "Notes toward a postcyberpunk manifesto." https://cyberpunk.asia/cp_project.php?txt=27&lng=fr. Accessed 2 Nov. 2020.
Robinson, Kim Stanley. 2018. *New York 2140*. London: Orbit.
Roth, Christopher. 2015. *HYPERSTITION Online Ansehen|Vimeo On Demand*. Accessed 2 Nov. 2020
Ryan, Marie-Laure. 1991. *Possible worlds, artificial intelligence and narrative theory*. Indiana University Press.
Ryan, Marie-Laure. 2001. *Narrative as virtual reality: Immersion and interactivity in literature and electronic media*. New. Baltimore: The Johns Hopkins University Press.
Schmeink, Lars. 2015. Cyberpunk and Dystopia: William Gibson, Neuromancer (1984). In *Dystopia, science fiction, post-apocalypse: Classics—New tendencies—Model interpretations*, ed. E. Voigts and A. Boller. Trier: WVT Wissenschaftlicher Verlag Trier.
Schröter, Jens. 2004. *Das Netz und die Virtuelle Realität: Zur Selbstprogrammierung der Gesellschaft durch die universelle Maschine*. Bielefeld: transcript.
Scott, Ridley. 1982. *Blade Runner*.
Shiner, Lewis. 1991. "Confessions of an ex-cyberpunk." *The New York Times*. https://www.nytimes.com/1991/01/07/opinion/confessions-of-an-excyberpunk.html. Accessed 2 Nov. 2020.
Green, Soylent. 1973. *Directed by Richard Fleischer*. USA: Metro-Goldwyn-Mayer.
Spielberg, Steven. 2002. *Minority Report*.
Sprawl Trilogy. n.d. William Gibson Wiki. https://williamgibson.fandom.com/wiki/Sprawl_trilogy. Accessed 2 Nov. 2020.
Stephenson, Neal. 1992. *Snow crash*. Barcelona: Ediciones Gigamesh.

Sterling, Bruce. 1986. *Mirrorshades: The cyberpunk anthology*. New York: Arbor House Pub Co.
Strauss, Claudia. 2006. The imaginary. *Anthropological Theory* 6 (3): 322–344. https://doi.org/10.1177/1463499606066891.
Suvin, Darko. 1972. On the poetics of the science fiction genre. *College English* 34 (3): 372–382. https://doi.org/10.2307/375141.
Suvin, Darko. 1979. *Poetik der Science-fiction. Zur Theorie und Geschichte einer literarischen Gattung*. Frankfurt a. M.: Suhrkamp.
Suvin, Darko. 1991. On Gibson and cyberpunk SF. In *Storming the reality studio: A casebook of cyberpunk & postmodern science fiction: A casebook of cyberpunk and postmodern science fiction*, ed. Larry McCaffery. New Durham: DUKE UNIV PR.
Taylor, Audrey Isabel, and S. Ekman. 2019. A practical application of critical world-building. *Foundation: The International Review of Science Fiction* 47.3 (131): 15–28.
Taylor, Charles. 2003. *Modern social imaginaries*. Durham: DUKE UNIV PR.
The Sprawl. n.d. William Gibson Wiki. https://williamgibson.fandom.com/wiki/The_Sprawl. Accessed 27 Feb. 2020.
Trench, Marianne. 1990. *Cyberpunk*. https://www.imdb.com/title/tt0398910/. Accessed 2 Nov. 2020
Ulibarri, Sarena, D. K. Mok, Jennifer Lee Rossman, Holly Schofield, Jaymee Goh, Wendy Nikel, Gregory Scheckler, and Julia K. Patt. 2018. *Glass and Gardens: Solarpunk Summers*. World Weaver Press.
von Stackelberg, Peter, and A. McDowell. 2015. What in the World? Storyworlds, Science Fiction, and Futures Studies. *Journal of Futures Studies*. https://jfsdigital.org/2015-2/vol-20-no-2-dec-2015/article/what-in-the-world-storyworlds-science-fiction-and-futures-studies/. Accessed 2 Nov. 2020.
Wachowski, Lana, and Wachowski, Lilly. 1999. *The Matrix*.
Waffender, Manfred. 1991. *Cyberspace—Ausflüge in Virtuelle Wirklichkeiten*. Reinbek: Rowohlt.
Wolf, Mark J. P. 2012. *Building imaginary worlds*. New York: Routledge.
Zaibatsu. n.d. William Gibson Wiki. https://williamgibson.fandom.com/wiki/Zaibatsu. Accessed 11 Mar. 2020.

Piazza Virtuale—The Public Sphere and Its Expansion Beyond the Physical

Hannah Glauner

Abstract

The artist collective Van Gogh TV developed an interactive television show that was broadcast live for a hundred days during *documenta IX* in 1992, testing the boundaries of communication systems in the virtual space from early on. When they named it *Piazza virtuale* they directly linked it to the town square, the Italian *piazza*, through the use of a topographical term which implies that there is a resemblance between the square's function in society and the function of the program on television. This essay will focus first on this idea that the town square is an ideal site for the manifestation of the public sphere by outlining social practices associated with it throughout history. Secondly, it will highlight how *Piazza virtuale* also provided a space for such social activities. When re-imagining them now, it becomes apparent that the program anticipated the essential role of the virtual space as a social platform today. With *Piazza virtuale*, the public sphere was expanded beyond the physical, and certain techniques were employed to encourage this expansion. The essay will search for visual representations of architecture within the television program which have been used throughout art history to provide authenticity to artificial spaces. Furthermore, linguistic techniques will be noted, such as the use of the name *Piazza virtuale*, as references to concepts that are known from our traditional environment.

Keywords

Public sphere · Metaphor · Piazza virtuale

H. Glauner (✉)
Humboldt-Universität zu Berlin, Berlin, Germany

Fig. 1 Piazza virtuale. Screenshot from "The Documentation," deutsch (1992), Material of the DFG research project "Van Gogh-TV. Multimedia-Documentation and Analysis of their Legacy", box 34, tape 371, TC: 00:13:33

The artist and musician John Cage died on 12 August 1992. Two days later, a memorial was held in his honor live on television (Fig. 1). More specifically, Cage was honored in the interactive TV program *Piazza virtuale*, which was broadcast for a hundred days throughout Europe as well America and Japan as part of *documenta IX* in Kassel. The artist collective Van Gogh TV developed the program in order to—as Berthold Brecht has already demanded in 1932 in his theory on the role of broadcasting at the time (Bühl 1997, p. 30)—turn the consumers of media into their producers. Therefore, it enabled the viewers to participate in the show, making it possible that they, even though physically separated, could make music together, chat, talk and remember John Cage during *Piazza virtuale*'s format *Classical Orchestra*.

In 1498, almost five hundred years earlier, the Florentine preacher, Girolamo Savonarola, was publicly executed at *Piazza della Signoria* in Florence on 23 May after a conflict with Alexander VI Borgia (Reinhardt 2013, p. 92). To this day a stone plate marks the exact location on the square where the execution took place.

In both cases, we are confronted with the public implementation of a social act. In one case an honoring commemoration is expressed, in the other a sentence is passed. Despite their similarity in nature, these acts are constituted in two different kinds of realms. One of them is an architecturally developed square which physically exists in an Italian city and the second is a virtual space, which should be considered as what we see through pictorial images (Ettlinger 2008, p. 2), yet both carry the term *piazza*, the denomination of the town square, in their names.

Often the attributes of places in a virtual space refer to characteristics of the physical space which serves as a starting point. When Van Gogh TV directly links *Piazza virtuale* to the square's function in society through the use of a topographical term, they create the idea that this function could also be fulfilled on the platform provided by the program. It becomes apparent here, that a metaphor is used to suggest that there is a resemblance between the television format and the town square. It elevates a traditional concept of social interaction to a new space and it operates as a means to make a new form of communication, which arose during the broadcasting time of *Piazza virtuale*, more approachable for viewers and participants. Even though its effect might be ambiguous in some cases, a metaphor can make something conceivable and therefore imaginable; television *as* a public square.

The town square will be considered in this essay as an ideal structure to give way to public debates or conflicts, making it suitable for the articulation of social practices as they have been pointed out before. These social activities had not yet found their place in virtual space by 1992. Van Gogh TV's *Piazza virtuale* provided that for the first time, thus challenging the possibility of virtual two-way communication from an early stage. To underline this aspect, the text will point out examples of social practices that were associated with the town square throughout history. These will then be related to social activity that happened on *Piazza virtuale* during *documenta IX*.

Furthermore, through the use of examples, the means which might have encouraged the expansion of the public sphere beyond the physical into the virtual space will be highlighted. Considered as such shall be the visual representation of architecture as well as the use of metaphors, and both serve the purpose of conveying an idea of a concept that we know from our traditional environment.

1 Public and Social Space

Essential for the execution of both acts which have been pointed out before, is the accessibility of the space in which they manifest themselves to the public. If this were not the case, their symbolic meaning would lose its effect. Hannah Arendt sees the origin of public space in the Greek *polis*. She makes a distinction between the private and the public in the ancient city-state by differentiating between the realm of the household on the one hand and the political sphere on the other. The latter would be the space that is common to every free citizen, strictly separated from the sphere of the *oikos*, which is inherent to each individual (Arendt 2011, pp. 62 f.). The transformation process from private to public would already apply to the act of speaking because an individual process would be made available to the general environment. The fact that conversations must first be expressed in order to be seen in public, demonstrates that their "being seen" demands the existence of a space in which they can manifest themselves. With this arises the assumption that the public space is not given but is first enlivened by the transformation process of inner and outer forms of expression (Nova and Jöchner 2010, p. 10).

The architectural historian Spiro Kostof (1993) considers the public sphere to be a place for the articulation of social conflicts as well as a place for the manifestation of social practices:

> The public space provides room for organized and communal events – celebrations, riots, ceremonies, public executions. That is why such venues express our common memory of past achievements as well as our shared rituals. In such places we will remember the dead who fell for us in a war. Perhaps we will also honor a ruler with a monument there. And perhaps one day we will gather there to tear it down again and condemn the honored one afterward (Kostof 1993, p. 124).

Kostof believes that this aspect, offering space for rituals, celebrations, or unrest, is realized in a privileged form in the main square of a European city. For him, the second criterion which makes it especially suitable for the constitution of publicity is the fact that it is easily and freely accessible, enabling chance encounters to take place (Kostof 1993, p. 124).

Likewise, the format *Piazza virtuale* was freely accessible to everyone, provided they had the necessary technical equipment, hence the virtual space can here fulfill the criteria of public space. However, at the time of the *documenta IX* in 1992, due to the state of technology, it was not yet possible to provide an interactive space for an unlimited number of participants at the same time; after all, available access lines were limited. On the other hand, a constant change of users enabled a lively and also coincidental exchange between a large number of different participants. And of course, not only participants but also viewers were able to become virtually involved in the events that took place on *Piazza virtuale* by tuning in at home to public broadcasts. Therefore, a large passive community could be observing, which in a broader context elevated the capacity of the virtual square to another level. A transformation from private to public took place since those who took part in the program made their statements and activities accessible to everyone through a publicly broadcast television program.

Coming back to the spatial formation of built architecture, it is assumed that it cannot be solely limited to the materialistic properties of a building or an urban structure. The intellectual content or the social function of a built structure shall from here on be referred to as social space. By referring directly to the physical—buildings, streets, or artworks on a square, for example—a direct link to social conventions (of the public) can be made through studying the design of the environment. Through this approach, a connection between constructed and social space, between the architectural space and its social function, can be established. Thus, the physically constructed space may also be understood as a passive inscription surface like a canvas, that reproduces social inclusion and exclusion. In this context, however, it would have a specific function: the visualization and legitimization of social structures. Through the inscription of an existing order into the architectural space, a process of habituation and naturalization would take place, making the social order appear legitimate (Hauser et al. 2011, pp. 14 f.).

The characteristic of having an architecturally, particularly suitable form as a place for the public, and at the same time having the ability to provide a platform for social space, can be ascribed to the town square. In the early 1990s, at a time when the internet was on the verge of becoming commercially viable, the possibilities of new virtual space concepts were tested on *Piazza virtuale*. In this context, it becomes apparent that it was also possible to provide an inscription surface for public and social space on television, thus in virtual space.

2 Contextualization of Social Practices on a Town Square and their Expansion into the Virtual Space

It will be shown that certain social practices that have been or are still being publicly carried out in a privileged form on a town square are referring to characteristics of places in the virtual space within the framework of *Piazza virtuale*. Three different practices that manifest themselves in the public sphere will be examined: Trade at the marketplace, entertainment on the public square, and political instrumentalization of the secular main square of a city.

2.1 Trade

The emergence of cities is often associated with the practice of trade. So-called market towns from pre-industrial times were founded or built especially for trade and often consisted only of long rows of houses that widened towards the center, thus creating a marketplace. There was usually one place in the city center which was reserved for trade: the Greek *agora*, the Roman *forum* or the medieval marketplace, which suggests that it was given a privileged form in the city's urban design, at least until the beginning of modern times[1] (Kostof 1993, pp. 92 ff.). Its central location indicates that good accessibility to the market is of great importance for the citizens, thus highlighting that its structure is inextricably linked to public activities and that the subsistence of trade is based on the existence of public interaction.

The ambiguity of the phrase *market*, which can be defined as a place as well as an institution, is reflected in the Latin term *mercatus*, which means both trade and the actual market. A market is a social structure for the exchange of goods, in which offers are evaluated and priced and compete with each other. Being defined as such, it can be concluded that economic activity is by its very nature social activity and that it, therefore, presupposes interpersonal practices. The market structure is determined by the two roles of buyer and seller who perform actual, not just potential, transactions. The two roles are associated with different interests, namely, to sell at a high price and to buy at a low price (Aspers 2015, p. 19). Hence the existence of a market would require at least three participants, a player on one side of the market facing at least two players on the other side, whose offers he can compare to one another (Simmel 1977). This requirement for a comparison of the offers again presupposes the public nature of a market, since in the private sector buyers usually have fewer possibilities to compare and the sellers have no competition.

Given that Van Gogh TV tested the boundaries of communication systems on television, it is not surprising that the team developed a program called *Marketplace* which was meant to be a platform for the selling, auctioning, and acquiring of goods in a virtual space. Participants could get in touch with each other via telephone to offer things or to purchase something they would be interested in. Their interactions would take place and be visualized on a simple screen layout.

---

[1] Although it was not until the fifteenth century that, "the systematization of the urban layout as a unity of function and aesthetic form was theoretically conceived" (Paul 1992, p. 26).

However, the program did not oversee any transactions and in fact didn't have any software to perform sales.[2]

Throughout the broadcasting time, the fact that capacities were limited and that it was not possible to buy or sell to the same extent as in a real marketplace quickly became apparent. There were few or possibly no offers from different providers, leaving viewers with no possibility to compare products, and therefore creating no competition between sellers. No buyer could examine or receive his or her purchase immediately, nor could the sellers receive their payment. It is not even certain whether the sales took place after the conversations on *Piazza virtuale*, because at the time of the broadcast there was no use of online transactions. At the moment of the sale, a purely honorable exchange of liabilities took place. The most important achievement of the *Marketplace* at that time is therefore not a complete shift of the market structure into the virtual space, but its opening for economic purposes. In this way, it was possible to show that trading in virtual space is possible at all. Even if the marketplace on *Piazza virtuale* was not yet able to compete with trading in the physical world at the time, the format predicted the rise of today's booming e-commerce industry.

2.2 Entertainment

An etching by Jacques Callot from 1617 shows a town square bordered by rows of buildings on three sites (Fig. 2). The church's facade on the left can be attributed to *Santa Croce* in Florence, thus revealing the identity of the square. In the foreground, occupying a large part of the center of the image, stands a drummer, seemingly on an organic elevation above the scenery behind him, with his legs spread wide apart and his upper body slightly twisted. He strikes out with his right arm, holding a drumstick, at the moment of capture. His gaze is directed to the upper right edge of the image, his eyes and mouth are open. In the middle of the square, a rectangular field is formed, surrounded by permeable barriers, behind which people seem to be observing the activities on the square. There, men are moving, both from the left as well as from the right side, from the back towards the center of the field, which is, though, covered by the drummer's body in the foreground. Yet visible is a ball on the left, on which the players' direction of movement seems to be concentrated, indicating that the image depicts a calcio match, a Florentine football event traditionally played on *Piazza Santa Croce* during the winter carnival period (Bredekamp 1993, p. 37).

---

[2]Benjamin Heidersberger (Interview, 24 August 2017).

Fig. 2 *Calcio in front of Santa Croce.* Jacques Callot 1617. Courtesy of prometheus Bildarchiv. URL: https://prometheus.uni-koeln.de/pandora/image/show/bochum_kgi-ac7a2f54b 5003bddc773aac73c5f534f111011b9

In his *Quattro libri dell'architettura* (1570), Andrea Palladio defines the square as a place that provides people with space to satisfy their needs. These needs would include practices such as trade or political discourse, as well as entertainment in the form of games, celebrations, or perhaps theatre (Palladio 1988, p. 246). The architect and theoretician Vitruvius (1991, p. 207) also writes about the design, in this case of marketplaces, that should be laid out to be capable of hosting gladiator games. The fact that entertaining events, such as calcio, take place on town squares can easily be explained by their topography since a field of similar dimensions to today's football fields would be difficult to build in narrow streets or along the waterfront (Bredekamp 1993, p. 17).

Bruno Nardini writes that *Piazza Santa Croce* in general became gradually a center of entertainment for the population (Baldini and Nardini 1985, p. 26), as the square was prepared for masses, sermons, and processions as well as tournaments and games. Calcio in Florence did not only serve a mere entertainment purpose, but its hosting had a representational function as well. It was inextricably linked to a magnificent staging of the entrance of the teams, which lasted about an hour and was as long as the actual performance of the sporting event. One of the most important matches took place demonstratively in 1530 during the siege of Florence by the troops of Charles V, which also marked the end of the republican calcio. Previously, any Florentine citizen was allowed to participate in the sport, but when Alessandro de' Medici came to power, participation in the game presupposed membership of the nobility, which resulted in intensive cultural promotion but also in the appropriation of the sport by the Medici family (Bredekamp 1993, p. 75). Nevertheless, calcio did not become a purely private event, because at least the Florentine people could not be deprived of the opportunity to watch the matches, and in some cases up to 40,000 guaranteed spectators from all social classes gathered for the events (Solmsdorf 2012, p. 42).

On *Piazza virtuale*, several program points can be detected which share a playful approach. At the beginning, there is the aforementioned *Classical Orchestra* (Fig. 1) wherein four participants were able to play virtual musical instruments together using the touchtone telephone keyboard. One voice line was available at the same time. In addition, ever-changing keywords were displayed on the screen, which showed live camera shots of a real place in a parallel window. An actual game called *Rotkäppchen-Spiel* was part of the agenda, developed by the project group *Universcity TV Zurich* which was an integral part of the *Piazzetta* format. The audience was able to control a Little Red Riding Hood figure and the figure of the wolf, thus symbolically taking over the identity of a different personality on screen by using the telephone's keypad, with the aim of bringing the two characters together (University TV Zürich 1992, p. 6). A similar approach to this appropriation of characters in virtual space can be found in the interactive format *Sarah & Daniel* (Fig. 3). It allowed the audience to control two actors who played the fictional lovers Sarah and Daniel whose moods and conversations were based on instructions given to them by the participants. Another player could also call in on the voice line to give them advice (Piazza virtuale. DFG research project, box 11, tape 108, 27. July 1992, TC: 00:06:16–00:20:17). Not only were the participants in those games on *Piazza virtuale* able to get together on the television screen, but hidden behind a character that does not correspond to the real physicality of the interacting person, they were given the opportunity to acquire a new identity, an early form of an avatar, in a different space.

Large staged celebrations or games, such as the calcio matches held in public town squares, cannot be compared in their tradition, scale, and also in the emotionality they evoke, with the playful approaches that took place on *Piazza virtuale*. However, the reason for this is strongly connected to developments in technology.

Fig. 3 Screenshot of Piazza virtuale. Material of the DFG research project "Van Gogh-TV. Multimedia-Documentation and Analysis of their Legacy", box 11, tape 108, 27. July 1992, TC: 00:13:21

Looking back on the format from today's perspective, one knows to what extent video and interactive games have grown, in regards of their potential for creating virtual worlds, but also their role in society, considering that gaming has become a profession, and of course in their impact on individuals, as well.

2.3 Political Instrumentalization

The development and political instrumentalization of *Piazza della Signoria* in Florence, which was mentioned in the introduction in relation to the public execution of Girolamo Savonarola (Fig. 4), shall be used as a brief example to demonstrate that it was also common to carry out social and political conflicts on a town square.

Fig. 4 *Execution of Savonarola*, Anonymous artist, fifteenth century. Courtesy prometheus Bildarchiv. URL: https://prometheus.uni-koeln.de/pandora/image/show/tuberlin-f99b0d415 2121e86f9324f30c0e49a10486a0abe

It took several centuries to complete the town square's design, prominently positioned in the heart of Florence, which was finished in stages, especially between 1200 and 1600. After the establishment of the Constitution of the Guilds in the thirteenth century, with the Signoria as the governing authority in Florence, a transformation of the urban cityscape began, which until then had been defined by private sectors in the form of towers and houses owned by noble families (Verspohl 1987, p. 368). But as the power of the people was becoming increasingly important, more and more public spaces suitable for their gathering had to be created. Therefore, the seat of government was excavated on the *Piazza della Signoria* in 1341 and the podium on the piazza, which until then had been made of wood, was built of stone (Braunfeld and Braunfels 2012, p. 104). This act signifies that it was widely understood that this square would be used to address the people publicly. Political principles and ideologies notably manifested themselves in the sculpture program on *Piazza della Signoria*, especially towards the end of the fifteenth century, at a time when the idea of the Republic was radicalized, but outside the city, various political interest groups pushed for an absolutist ruled territorial state. The Republic, feeling unstable, therefore recognized the need to propagate the ideal image of a republican citizen using for this purpose the symbolic effect of the installation of artworks in public space (Verspohl 1987, p. 319). Just to point out one of many examples I'm referring to Donatello's *Judith and Holofernes* (approx. 1457–1464) which was brought to the square after the expulsion of the Medici family. The people of Florence took the sculpture from the gardens of the family's palace, taking it away from their private property, to place it on the secular main square of the city. This act represents an eerily symbolic articulation of their triumph over the Medici. On the pedestal, they added the inscription: "This example of public interest was installed by the citizens in 1495" (Verspohl 1987, p. 319). Since this victory had to be publicly displayed, the main square in front of *Palazzo Vecchio* provided the ideal site for such demonstration.

How much room for political instrumentation or social debates can an interactive television program provide? Van Gogh TV definitely broadcast several formats enabling participants to publicly state their opinions and discuss them with others. The *Coffeehouse* was a platform for genuine interpersonal exchange. Before the program would start, it would already be mentioned in the introduction that, "here you can hang out, chat up, politicize, argue, exaggerate and release steam" (Piazza virtuale. DFG research project, box 8, tape 74, 17. July 1992, TC: 00:57:56). Four telephone lines converged for the *Coffehouse* and four modem users could join the communication network. The incoming faxes were displayed in a separate window on the screen, which, however, could also be connected to a public entry point in Kassel. Although most of the criticism which has been expressed against the program, was pointing out the lack of sophisticated conversations, there have still been some lively debates on social and political issues as well as on current events.

When in August 1992 right-wing extremist riots against a reception center for refugees and a house for former Vietnamese contract workers took place in Rostock, the topic arose on *Piazza virtuale* where participants would state their different opinions. Karel Dudesek recapitulates the public discourse in an interview and states that the programs themselves would reflect all possible aspects of society:

The broadcast's openness is a part of it. These open structures of communication should be taken advantage of. Only in communication, only with the confrontation within the community, within society, can one begin to reflect. In regard to the events in Rostock about a week ago, people showed themselves to be pro and contra and we see that everything comes out in the broadcasts. One could say that everyone who is pro should be muzzled the moment they say 'Rostock, yes!'-pow, I throw them out. All those who criticize the events in Rostock get onto the broadcasts and have a platform on which they can express themselves. But, no! Everyone must have an outlet for their views so that both groups come together in a public critic. This is an essential discovery we have made in this project, that you have to put forward total social developments and social strata. And that they are not censored or deprived of the right to speak. This is to proof whether or not they can stand their ground through this social filter. We have to risk this in society, and this is what we do. (Piazza virtuale. DFG research project, box 34, tape 371, The Documentation, TC: 00:14:42–00:16:11)

The establishment of an open space for free speech formed a crucial basis for the emergence of broad public discourses that would not differentiate between sender and receiver, as it was the case with media such as radio or non-interactive television. Hans Magnus Enzensberger's media theory states that "the development from a mere distribution medium to a communication medium is not a technical but a political problem" (Bühl 1997, p. 289).

Another event which took place during the hundred days of broadcasting should be pointed out because it reflects how much impact the discourses in the program were already expected to have. This is related to censorship, of which Karel Dudesek is speaking in the previous quote and which, after all, was only not resorted to as long as there was no serious reason for it. Yet, the responsible institutions did see a reason for it as soon as someone called in and encouraged the audience to murder Helmut Kohl. Since then, Kathrin Brinkmann from ZDF has been responsible for operating a censor button in seemingly critical moments during the live broadcasts (Fig. 5).[3]

The characteristic of a public square, being a suitable space for political instrumentalization, was highlighted for the first time in virtual space on *Piazza virtuale*. For unlike the encounter and interaction on a town square, the interactive virtual space provided the opportunity to express an opinion anonymously and to mobilize viewers of the program without openly having to stand for your convictions. What might be even more crucial is that it also enabled one to reach a significantly larger number of people, who above all did not need to be in the same place, but could be spread all over the world, as long as they were able to access the program. That this form of reaching out to and interacting with the public would

---

[3] Benjamin Heidersberger (Interview, 24 August 2017).

Fig. 5 Screenshot of Piazza virtuale. Material of the DFG research project "Van Gogh-TV. Multimedia-Documentation and Analysis of their Legacy", box 11, tape 108, 27. July 1992, TC: 01:08:18

especially later be instrumentalized to the highest extent, was already foreseen at the time.

3 Architecture and Metaphors in Virtual Space

If one recapitulates the observations which have been made previously, it can certainly be stated that some social structures that manifested themselves on the town square can also be observed on *Piazza virtuale*. In order to make this possible, Van Gogh TV used a range of techniques to encourage the expansion of social practices into a new, virtual space.

The role of architecture as a means to frame an image is ubiquitous in art history. Since the invention of perspective in art at the time of the Renaissance, one intention in the creation of visual images has been to give an experienceable, illusionist authenticity to artificial spaces.

In the ceiling fresco *Triumph of St. Ignatius of Loyola* (1691–1694) by Andrea Pozzo, which is on the barrel vault of the nave of the church *Sant'Ignazio* in Rome, painted columns and arches reach upwards above the last pillars of the built architecture of the church (Fig. 6). Angels and various figures related to Christian faith seem to float in the air, surrounding St. Ignatius of Loyola who is placed centered on a cloud. As Oliver Grau (1999, p. 44) points out, "With the virtuoso and scientific use of the means of illusion, Pozzo understood how to merge the real with the figurative architecture and to continue into the sky – as if the sky and the church room were one and the same reality".

Leon Battista Alberti (2013, p. 19) famously makes the comparison between a painting and an open window revealing a view for the spectator. Its transparency would enable the projection of three-dimensional bodies onto a two-dimensional support. The medium's reference to the idea of the vista as a symbolic duplication of reality suggests that the representation of architectural elements might increase the experience of physical space in the form of its depicted doppelganger. In Edward Hopper's *Night Windows* (1928) an illuminated interior is dramatically emphasized against the dark night (Fig. 7). The viewer looks at a building's façade, but what becomes more apparent is what is behind it. The intimate scenery with an anonymous woman seems like an entirely different world that is visible through but is also inscribed in the transparent surfaces of the three windows.

The pictorial duplication of reality has been perfected more and more with the development of new technologies. Since the end of the nineteenth century, spaces, objects, and movements could be visualized and simulated even more realistically through photography and later film. Implemented to imitate but also to challenge the perception of reality and to open up a specific view into the artificial space, structures that underline the spatial effect of the illusory medium were regularly incorporated in images. It could, therefore, be argued that after the transition from moving to interactive images, figurative architecture would still be used as the raw material to build virtual spaces.

However, this development, from movement to interaction, meant new opportunities as well as new challenges for those who create or are confronted with images. The border, which the screen used to create between the user and the machine, vanished and one could navigate interactively in the space behind the screen. This enabled the virtual space to also become a social space. When a pictorial, non-interactive space was constructed in our previous examples and figurative architecture was part of it, then it could have a merely visual, potentially immersive effect on the viewers, challenging their perception of body and medium. This might of course also cause personal or social consequences. However, its nature is confronting and representational. At first it shows, and then we see. At the moment a virtual space becomes interactive, it becomes shapeable. The interactive surface of the screen, in opposition to the moving one, would usually cause the static viewer to react to what he or she is confronted with which might cause

Fig. 6 Triumph of St. Ignatius of Loyola. Andrea Pozzo 1691–1694. Courtesy of prometheus Bildarchiv. URL: https://prometheus.uni-koeln.de/de/image/digidia-250920d7e6a7172e402445664c130374b45a6657

Fig. 7 Night Windows. Edward Hopper 1928. Courtesy of prometheus Bildarchiv. URL: https://prometheus.uni-koeln.de/de/image/digidia-250920d7e6a7172e40244566 4c130374b45a6657

another reaction to the display. This interplay is closely linked to the simultaneous stimulation of other senses. During *Piazza virtuale* viewers are also exposed to acoustic stimuli when having conversations or playing music together. Accordingly, the pictorial space has now the potential to offer a platform for the viewer's mobilized body to act in and is thereby changing the requirements for pictorial representation in virtual space: it is not necessarily expected to find a duplication of reality, but an environment that lets one behave to an extent as if they were in reality.

Architectural representations could also be found to a certain extent on the screens during *documenta IX*. Hans Belting (2011, p. 24) refers to today's screen as the archetype of the surface of Alberti's symbolic window. And even within the screen's architectural design—a term which can as easily be applied to the construction of virtual spaces considering for example that Microsoft founder Bill Gates holds the title of *chief software architect* (Warnke 2008, p. 83)—Van Gogh TV has made use of several different windows to visually separate the distinct forms of communication from each other, or for example, to establish a connection to one of the *Piazettas* in form of video recordings of a scenery in physical space. In the framework of the program point *Moby Dicks Eye*, one window was connected to actual research stations and ships on the ocean which in this case does look similar to a ship's porthole (Fig. 8). The use of these windows, or 'portals' must have been an essential element to help the participants, who were not used to being able to navigate in virtual space, to archive an understanding of the communication network, but also a feeling for the different spaces which were being brought together in one.

However, not so many doppelgangers of spatial structures which are commonly known from the physical environment were visually represented on *Piazza virtuale*, and an actual square was only visible in videos of the *Piazzettas*. Yet, it must be remembered that the realistic duplication of physical space through the form of interactive images would not have been possible with the technical equipment of the time. The establishment of a framework for a functioning communication system on television might have therefore required an interplay with topographical metaphors as a reference to physical space.

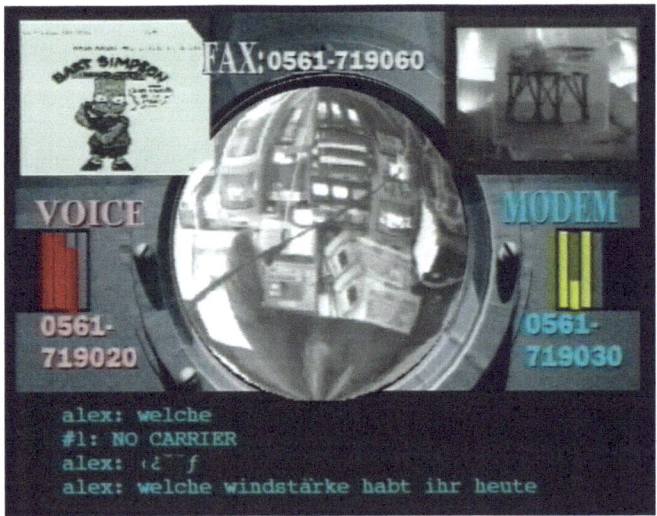

Fig. 8 Piazza virtuale. Screenshot of "The Documentation, deutsch" (1992). Material of the DFG research project "Van Gogh-TV. Multimedia-Documentation and Analysis of their Legacy", Screenshot box 34, tape 371, TC: 00:12:49

In fact, several of Van Gogh TV's program points on *Piazza virtuale* were based on metaphors. The format's title, which means 'virtual square', is making use of a topographical term. Just as the *Coffehouse*, the *Marketplace*, *Medialandscape*, or the *Piazzetta*, the latter meaning the 'small square'.

At this point, the visionary and completely new approach of the format shall be recalled. It was the first time a live television show became an interactive program. The press wrote about "the vision of television of the future" (Unknown Author 1992, p. 76). *Der Spiegel* predicted a complete change of the media world: "If nothing goes wrong, then it will finally become true what critics and theorists have been dreaming of for as long as radio has existed: The audience breaks the power of the stations, the viewers make their own programs, the screen becomes permeable for everyone who has something to say" (Seidl 1992, p. 268).

Benjamin Heidersberger recalls that for the participants on *Piazza virtuale*, maneuvering within the program was a learning process: "In the beginning, our first few transmissions, to tell the truth, were a bit chaotic. People were just phoning simply to see how things worked, just saying: 'Hello, I'm Peter calling from Stuttgart', and so on and so forth" (Piazza virtuale. DFG research project, box 34, tape 371, The Documentation, 00:04:33–00:05:10). Thus, if one looks at the media competence of the participants on *Piazza virtuale* at the beginning of the 1990s without understanding it in the context of modern interactive media, it is clear that there were difficulties, at least initially, to react in a reflective and considered manner to the format. A careful approach to something new is part of the norm. However, getting to know an illusion, leads also to the fact that the person learns to deal with a new medium (Grau and Keil 2005, p. 80).

In this regard, the use of metaphors was an important instrument to expand social practices into the virtual space, especially at a time when a familiar environment for the participants could not yet be created visually on screen. As a reference to concepts we know from our traditional environment or even from other media, they let us imagine what new concepts *could* be about. Even though their symbolic meaning can be inexplicit in some instances, they have been involved significantly in establishing a co-existence of the public sphere in virtual space. In today's internet culture one is still surrounded by spatial metaphors when navigating in *chat rooms* or *forums*. Martin Warnke (2008, pp. 83 f.) states that communicative conditions are easier to understand in their symbolism if one gets involved in [crooked] metaphors. When calling the format *Piazza virtuale* and other parts of the program *Marketplace* or *Coffeehouse*, language naturally conveys an image of a town square or a café, and just like it has been done in this essay, viewers re-imagine the social practices which were associated with these places.

References

Arendt, Hannah. 2011. *Vita activa oder Vom tätigen Leben*. München: Piper (First published in 1958).
Alberti, Leon Battista. 2013. *Della Pittura – Über die Malkunst*, 4th ed. Darmstadt: Wissenschaftliche Buchgesellschaft (First published in 1435/36).
Aspers, Patrik. 2015. *Märkte*. Wiesbaden: Springer VS.
Baldini, Umberto, and Bruno Nardini, eds. 1985. *Santa Croce: Kirche, Kapellen, Kloster, Museum*. Stuttgart: Urachhaus.
Belting, Hans. 2011. *Bild Anthropologie. Entwürfe für eine Bildwissenschaft*, 4th ed. München: Fink.
Braunfels, Wolfgang. 2012. *Mittelalterliche Stadtbaukunst in der Toskana*, 7th ed. Berlin: Mann.
Bredekamp, Horst. 1993. *Florentiner Fußball: Die Renaissance der Spiele: Calcio als Fest der Medici*. Frankfurt a. M.: Campus.
Bühl, Achim. 1997. *Die virtuelle Gesellschaft. Ökonomie, Kultur und Politik im Zeichen des Cyperspace*. Opladen: Westdeutscher Verlag.
Ettlinger, Or. 2008. *In search of architecture in virtual space: An introduction to the virtual space theory*. Ljubljana: University of Ljubljana/Faculty of Architecture.
Grau, Oliver. 1999. *Virtuelle Kunst in Geschichte und Gegenwart. Visuelle Strategien*. Berlin: Reimer.
Grau, Oliver, and Andreas Keil, eds. 2005. *Mediale Emotionen. Zur Lenkung von Gefühlen durch Bild und Sound*. Frankfurt a. M.: Fischer Taschenbuch Verlag.
Hauser, Susanne, Christa Kamleithner, and Roland Meyer, eds. 2011. *Architekturwissen. Grundlagentexte aus den Kulturwissenschaften. Vol. 1: Zur Ästhetik des sozialen Raumes*. Bielefeld: transcript.
Kostof, Spiro. 1993. *Die Anatomie der Stadt. Geschichte städtischer Strukturen*. Frankfurt a. M.: Campus.
Nova, Alessandro, and Cornelia Jöchner, eds. 2010. *Platz und Territorium. Urbane Struktur gestaltet politische Räume*. Berlin: Deutscher Kunstverlag.
Palladio, Andrea. 1988. *Die vier Bücher zur Architektur*. Zürich: Verlag für Architektur Artemis (First published in 1570).
Paul, Jürgen. 1992. Funktion und Gestalt von Plätzen im Mittelalter. In *La Piazza. Kunst und öffentlicher Raum – Geschichte – Realitäten – Visionen*, ed. Gisela Febel and Gerhart Schröder, 14–29. Stuttgart: Hatje.
Reinhardt, Volker. 2013. *Geschichte von Florenz*. München: Beck.
Seidl, Claudius. 1992. Die imaginäre Piazza. 'Piazza virtuale' – Die Zukunft des Fernsehens. *Der Spiegel*, 21.
Simmel, Georg. 1977. *Philosophie des Geldes. Gesammelte Werke, Bd. 1*, 7th ed. Berlin: Duncker & Humblot.
Solmsdorf, Christopher. 2012. *Vom Strohball zur Bundesliga. Der Weg vom historischen Ballspiel bis in die Neuzeit*. Hamburg: Diplomica.
University TV Zürich. 1992. Ein Beitrag von University TV Zürich für Piazza virtuale an der Documenta IX. Zürich – Kassel 13.06.1992–20.09.1992.
Unknown author. 1992. Binärer Bilderofen. *Mac News*, September, S. 76.

Verspohl, Franz-Joachim. 1987. Der Platz als politisches Gesamtkunstwerk. In *Kunst. Die Geschichte ihrer Funktionen*, ed. Werner Busch and Peter Schmook, 307–333. Weinheim: Quadriga.
Vitruvius Pollio, Marcus. 1991. *Zehn Bücher über Architektur*. Darmstadt: Wissenschaftliche Buchgesellschaft.
Warnke, Martin. 2008. Der Raum des Cyberspace. In *welt[stadt]raum*, ed. Annett Zinsmeister, 81–104. Bielefeld: transcript.

Videos

Piazza virtuale. DFG research project "Van Gogh-TV. Multimedia-Documentation and Analysis of their Legacy", box 34, tape 371, The Documentation, deutsch.
Piazza virtuale. DFG research project "Van Gogh-TV. Multimedia-Documentation and Analysis of their Legacy", box 8, tape 74, 17. July 1992.
Piazza virtuale. DFG research project "Van Gogh-TV. Multimedia-Documentation and Analysis of their Legacy", box 11, tape 108, 27. July 1992.
Benjamin Heidersberger (Interview, 24 August 2017).

Reimagining *Piazza virtuale*—A Conversation with Van Gogh-TV

Christoph Ernst, Jens Schröter, Karel Dudesek, Benjamin Heidersberger, Salvatore Vanasco, and Mike Hentz

> Questions: Christoph Ernst & Jens Schröter
>
> Answers: Karel Dudesek, Benjamin Heidersberger, Mike Hentz, Salvatore Vanasco

Abstract

In this interview, the members of the media artist group Van Gogh-TV provide insight into the production of their interactive television project *Piazza virtuale* at the documenta IX art exhibition in Kassel/Germany 1992. The original idea, the conceptual and technical challenges, the reactions at the time and the follow-up project *Service area a.i.* (1994) are discussed. The interview

C. Ernst (✉) · J. Schröter
Rheinische Friedrich-Wilhelms-Universität, Bonn, Germany
E-Mail: cernst@uni-bonn.de

J. Schröter
E-Mail: schroeter@uni-bonn.de

K. Dudesek
Wien, Austria
E-Mail: karel.dudesek@me.com

B. Heidersberger
Berlin, Germany
E-Mail: benjamin@ponton-lab.de

S. Vanasco
Berlin, Germany
E-Mail: salvatore.vanasco@xailabs.de

© The Author(s), under exclusive license to Springer Fachmedien Wiesbaden GmbH, part of Springer Nature 2021
C. Ernst and J. Schröter (eds.), *(Re-)Imagining New Media*, Neue Perspektiven der Medienästhetik, https://doi.org/10.1007/978-3-658-32899-3_8

also addresses the legacy of the project and its relevance in the current media landscape.

Question 1

Christoph Ernst & Jens Schröter: As you know, we are working on the topic of imaginative processes of the much-cited "new media" from around 1990. We will start right there with the first question: Catchwords of that time such as "cyberspace" or "virtual reality" were undoubtedly suggestive and also appear in the *Piazza virtuale* context to a large extent. What was your relationship to such terms? Were catchwords like these used more instrumentally as a means to an end, or was virtuality, for example, also something like a "leitmotif" for the development of *Piazza virtuale* or the earlier Project *Hotel Pompino*?

Karel Dudesek: Two years prior to *Piazza virtuale* 1990 at the *Ars Electronica*, *Van Gogh TV* produced its first cyber TV project, which was broadcast on 3sat throughout Europe: *Hotel Pompino*, with virtual sets and virtual stages (blue-green screen). The participants were able to enter the virtual hotel and, by means of hand gestures captured by tracking cameras, walk through the entire virtual building and enter a wide variety of virtual rooms with different themes. *Van Gogh TV* regularly visited various developer companies in Silicon Valley and had regular exchanges with several VR evangelists. Moreover, we were also aware

---

M. Hentz
Berlin, Germany
E-Mail: metronam@gmx.net

of the first interactive television project in Orlando, which was run by SGI and Time Warner, although this was not real interactive television, but only VOD—Video on demand. These contacts naturally inspired us and our ideas to think further than the industry in our concept development, because after all, as artists we were not exposed to commercial pressure.
Technically, *Hotel Pompino* was indeed a great challenge, because we had to combine low tech with high tech. In addition to the virtual sets, the audience in this project was already included live through call-in and text chat. *Hotel Pompino* opened up a completely new universe for us in terms of virtuality and telecommunication in combination with performance art.

Benjamin Heidersberger: In 1992 I wrote: "There will be a media coffee house, a virtual piazza, which, like the mediterranean piazza, will unfold its centripetal forces. ... the public in the electronic medium ... it can be reached in form of telepresence *via* the various media networks that Ponton is exploring today and which are accessible to everyone. Streets, windows and doors open, faces and voices appear. People will talk, play, type; images, sounds, texts merge into a new surface, which is broadcasted and can be experienced in many places" (Heidersberger 1992, p. 141). By 1991/1992 at the latest, virtuality was a clear objective for us.
Although the origins of immersive artificial environments are older (Evans and Sutherland-Company 1968), the term "cyberspace" only became known with William Gibson's *Newromancer* (1984). I read

the book later in the 1990s. I got acquainted with virtual reality in spring 1990 during a research trip for MACup in Silicon Valley (see Heidersberger 1991). I had read about cyberspace in Taiwan (probably in Mondo 2000) and flew there right away. I would deny an orientation on fixed notions in our projects, it was rather a sleepwalking certainty to do the right thing at the right time. Dwarves on the shoulders of giants, as Newton said. Sure, we picked up ideas that were in the air, and even threw some in the air that others picked up. Brian Eno visited us in 1987, John Perry Barlow, William Gibson and Captain Crunch in Linz in 1990 at *Hotel Pompino*, and the results of our research could be seen at festivals like the Ars Electronica and in broadcasts.

This research was unique in its condensation of visions, talents, materials, technologies, possibilities and goodwill. On the one hand, the time was ripe to close the communication loop, to move towards interactivity, but on the other hand, the time was also innocent, there was no advertising, no business model, no exit strategy, no safety net. Authenticity was our signature.

I had a hard time with the philosophers of the time (especially the French ones). I felt it was more productive to solder cables to connect devices to create new functions, develop circuits and work with the incredibly talented programmers and graphic designers like Christian Wolff ("der Hacker" [the hacker]), and Ole Lütjens, whom we had on the team. Philosophy always came afterwards; it was more the door to intellectual discourse

	with others. Especially since most philosophers couldn't program or solder (with the exception of Friedrich Kittler) and had little connection to practice. I vaguely remember an unfortunate discussion with Vilém Flusser about "Regenschirm, Fallschirm, Bildschirm." He had once managed a radio and transformer factory in Brazil and I would have expected him to be more on the practical side.
	The discussion with like-minded people was not always easy either. "So you spent millions just to fart in a trumpet", DeeDee Halleck from Paper Tiger TV accused us after a presentation of *Hotel Pompino* in New York.
Salvatore Vanasco:	My vision for *Piazza virtuale* was to bring life into the square of the cathode tube. The Piazza Reale, from the Renaissance conception of cities and their development, saw the piazza as a place with an expanded social functional space such as this.
	This diversity motivated me to provide concepts and communication processes with points of interaction in order to stimulate immediate concentration and resonance in addition to the communicative activity. Much more than VR or other trends, I was driven by the linguistic and creative possibilities of multimedia and coupled interactivity.
Mike Hentz:	Our contacts with virtual reality date back 30 years by now: In 1990/91 the first *Van Gogh TV*-tour to America took place, during which several TV live shows and lectures were held. But we also experienced interesting personal encounters. Benjamin and I met Jaron Lanier, one of the pioneers of virtual reality. We also had

the opportunity to visit the NASA-Labs and the *Electronic Café* in Los Angeles. There, we had the opportunity to try out VR-goggles for the first time. I was not very enthusiastic about them: for one, because of the great technical effort required, the very high costs at the time, and furthermore they completely separated the user from "reality".

We had heated discussions among the group about our understanding of VR. Originally, VR was developed in a military context as a training program for pilots, captains etc. The goal was to enable training for reality by simulating reality. Diverging from this origin, we came to agree that everything was "reality". We did not want to leave room for the speculations and the hype around the term "virtual reality". Along the lines of: "Plastic is from nature—so it is a natural thing."

Important reflections in this context for me at that time were the possibilities of further development of the human brain. Considering the issue that parts of our brain capacity are unused, an expansion should be considered essential and sensible. I have regarded "Telepathic Communication" as one of the first possibilities for further development of the human brain. Because technical media and human sensory perception are closely related.

In the present, realization of "telepathy" takes place through prostheses. Following the definition of Marshall McLuhan, according to which media are the sensory prostheses of human beings, a prosthetic expansion of the body can be achieved in this way. In this sense, SMS, mobile phones and the internet are prostheses of the brain. Even microchips implanted in the brain are already a reality. VR has also found its commercial application in the world of video and online games. But in contrast to its original use as a means of training for reality, VR today is mainly used as an escape from reality into other realities.

Question 2

Christoph Ernst & Jens Schröter: Let us circle back to the keyword of "re-imagining"—i.e. imagining something "anew" or "again." Looking at a project such as *Piazza virtuale* from a contemporary perspective is exciting, simply because the idea of interactive television as a medium with a promising future—after the interim triumph of the WWW—seems rather foreign to us today. Which is of course a problematic perspective, since you couldn't foresee it at the time. How has the idea of "interactive television" as a medium of the future presented itself? What were the fascinating points for you about this vision of interactive television?

Karel Dudesek: We radically wanted the television program to be run mainly by the so-called viewer. It was clear relatively early that this was the goal. The audience makes its own program, and live. We realized that this would be a long learning process during the *Piazza virtuale* in Kassel,[1] not only for us, but also for the people in front of the screens. The conditioning

---

[1] Reference to *d*ocumenta IX, which took place from June 13th to 20th September 1992 in Kassel.

of people as passive consumers is still practiced today intensively with all means. If necessary, with chemicals or violence. The state and industry need apathetic citizens and not active or even interactive participants and certainly not people who think and communicate. *Piazza virtuale* was the first step towards liberation from these constraints, *Piazza virtuale* was a psychotherapeutic experience for people in front of the screens. They were—as they were used to regular television program—very much unaccustomed to being able to participate. It was irritating for many at the beginning that nobody guided their first steps, no presenter, no entertainer, most of them fell as if blind into a dark hole and shouted "Hello, hello, is anyone there?". There were many discussions among the team whether and how this banality should be addressed, some wanted to entertain in a traditional way again, as moderators do to bridge the naturally arising boredom. For entertainment television, boredom is a shame, a catastrophe. I think that within the program of *Piazza virtuale* there was partly boredom, emptiness, not knowing what they should do now, what they actually want to do there, an important realization and part of the decoupling of role-playing from commercial television. Where everyone has to be kept in a permanent trance as if on drugs. This is what the professionally trained supervisors—moderators, like Gottschalk etc.—are used for, to prevent the viewer from thinking, from self-reflection. The mass stupefaction, practiced for many years until today *via* ZDF with Scooter

	or DJ BoBo (by the way, the most horrible thing I have ever seen on German television), is actually the primary problem for all of us, because in this way millions of people are excluded from the creative thinking process and collectively degenerate through rhythmic hand clapping. Environmental problems, health problems—we have those because people are prevented from working on them. There are too few people who participate in remedying these negative factors.
Benjamin Heidersberger:	In the 1990s, interactive television from an industry perspective was the possibility of having pre-produced and non-interactive content (then Disney, now Netflix) shown on one's own television set and remote-controlled *via* a back channel, possibly changing the camera angle or calling up alternative scenes (e.g. Time Warner, Inc. in Orlando/Florida).
	This one-to-many distribution is initially related to the nature of radio waves, which also represent an economic distribution structure in cable networks, and with which existing content can be exploited commercially in multiple ways. Digitalization makes the leap from simultaneous broadcasting to time-shifted individual consumption possible, but at the same time deprives television of its function as a campfire and the "Leitmedium" of society. In this time of unidirectional pressure from the transmitter to the receiver, Van Gogh TV enters with the promise to turn the receiver into the transmitter as well. "In the future, everyone will be world-famous for 15 minutes," said Andy Warhol in 1968, "I'm on TV," said the Van Gogh TV

viewer who, after three weeks of dialing in, finally managed to "get through". Communication itself becomes the content, the communication with many others. My theory is, that every trend comes back every 25 years. The problems remain the same. *Zoom* as the contemporary answer to Corona struggles with the same problems as we did back in 1992: How many people can fit on one screen? What is the communication metaphor? How do you deal with echoes?

A little technical excursion: The demand of Brecht's radio theory to turn every receiver into a transmitter is actually redundant, because the oscillator of the heterodyne receiver (patented in 1918) is already a transmitter which was happily used to locate pirate listeners/viewers. What is less known: the transmissions of one's own heterodyne receiver, which is traditionally built up with a variable capacitor and an inductance, are modulated with acoustic room events (e.g. of conversations) and can be received even outside of the room (e.g. by secret services).

Salvatore Vanasco: I was displeased with the idea of television as a "*Leitmedium*" and the abuse of media monopolies in providing information, directing the social narrative and thereby controlling the population. The ensuing societal design of a crowd that is to be controlled and is not itself responsible, was based at the time on a theorem of communicative competence. My goal or wish was the democratization of media, the abolition of the sender-receiver paradigm, towards a television as the actual social democratic place of action. My

	intention was to change the "Leitmedium", but to keep it valid as a "Leitmedium". In other words, to convert every television viewer into a communicator, in order to break the power of the media to shape opinion, to give every citizen the opportunity to develop a democratic relationship towards the sender-receiver ratio, and to be able to take more care of their own and to evaluate the reflections gained in exchange with others. Some of the cultural mechanics applied in *Piazza virtuale* were tested, reflected and implemented in the *Piazza virtuale's* communication toolbox in the field of multi-user telephony and the first Internet services (Multicast, Whois, Finger, BBS, etc.).
Mike Hentz:	The desire for a mobile studio and broadcasting studio had long matured among us and originated in the *MinusDeltaT*-times. But in the 1980s during the *Stone-Project* in countries like Iran, Turkey and Pakistan it was not possible to broadcast free radio formats.[2] As an alternative, we produced travel reports for almost a year, which were broadcast on Austrian radio every Friday in the program *Musikbox*. Unlike *Van Gogh TV*, however, we were a closed group in the *MinusDeltaT Stone-Project*. The first *Ponton* Bus in 1987 was then a mobile, open atelier.
	Our vision of television was defined by the fact that television was actually designed to be interactive. Even the first transmission of images from Berlin to Leipzig in

---

[2] In 1982 the artist group Minus Delta T started The [Stone]-Project: A 5 1/2 ton granite stone was to be transported from Wales to Asia. (Source: https://www.kunstforum.de/artikel/minus-delta-t/).

1925 by Karolus was interactive and intended for communication. But due to the state monopoly, radio and television were later limited to a one-way information system.

Our ideas, on the other hand, to work with new media and to implement interactive television did not develop from the technical side. It was primarily an artistic motivation and approach. It was also always especially important for us to be independent of production means. If we look at the situation at the end of the 1980s, almost no live programs were produced on public television—presumably out of fear of losing control over the program's interpretative sovereignty. This monopoly on content and, in addition, on finance by the public broadcasters strengthened our desire for independent means of production and communication.

At that time, we differentiated between individual art and collective art. We placed the latter above individual art. We were interested in art that developed through communication between collectives in newly created networks. The idea of a network existed at that time only in a scientific context. Therefore, we transferred this model into our artistic group work. We developed a horizontal hierarchical structure to avoid the classical vertical hierarchy. The means of communication and creative production should be accessible to all members of the group. The group work was a pool of creativity in the artistic process. The collective studio and the transparency of the artistic process ultimately had the same priority for us as the finished end product, the broadcast.

Through diversity of opinion in a creative pool we saw the possibilities of synergetic and practical learning, research and development of new formats of communication art. By developing together, all group members had an overview of the content. Our different professions and areas of expertise, united in a horizontally hierarchical group, gave us many new practical experiences and made us capable of acting. Through these synergies we were ahead of many groups, labs and other structures.

The use and combination of different media was always a concern for us. There were trainings in the respective special fields, but networking or cooperation was almost non-existent. However, years of working with polymedia or multimedia in the group have allowed us to develop a lot of practical experience and new skills.

Our idea of a subjective artistic expression, however, was contrary to the established formats of the public broadcasters. The criticism was that we were not professional enough: not trained for it, no experts, not earnest and serious enough, qualitatively insufficient, etc. We had to defend ourselves against various criticisms, e.g. that our artistic and intellectual standards were too low ("*Hallo TV*").

In part, we were dissatisfied with the artistically and aesthetically still very weak results of the programs as well. According to our ideal of perfection at that time, we had achieved perhaps 30%. We were aware that much was still missing. And we suffered a lot from that. On the other hand, our priority was the new system of a communicative and creative democratic program. We had forbidden ourselves to interfere in these processes and merely provided the framework of the program. Katrin Brinkmann was appointed by the TV-station 3sat to block unconstitutional and inhumane content.

With *Piazza virtuale*, we had many more ideas and projects that we could not realize due to lack of time or financial reasons. These included, for example, the idea of an interactive monument or educational and orientation programs.

Unfortunately, Beuys' theory that "everyone is an artist" turned out to be a horrible and, unfortunately, vulgar triviality. The invited artists and piazzettas let themselves be dazzled by the myth of television, especially in the early stages, and predominantly pursued self-expression. They partly ignored the other participants of the show, so that the interaction between them was very tedious—if it happened at all.

However, the practice led to a self-learning effect in the chat rooms and in the programs. The chat-communities got used to each other and the quality improved. The initial unprofessionalism produced many "Piazza Virtualists" at the end of the project. This new practical experience with interactivity during the three-month *Piazza virtuale*-project was its real success. Until then, interactive art had mainly been based on expensive, symbolic art installations presented at media festivals.

A later analysis by Van Gogh TV showed that with the then emerging medium Internet an opportunity was missed to design an attractive and effective school television. The young people of the time could recite 300 names of Pokémon off the cuff, but contents of the classic educational canon were alien to them. Here, the possibilities of interactive television would certainly have provided an opportunity to increase the attractiveness of Goethe and co.

Due to the social upheavals and technical innovations of the 1990s, established value systems collapsed and concepts of quality shifted. Our concept back then of initiating self-learning processes and expecting a creative result can no longer be evaluated in the same way today. Interactive television has been overtaken by the video game culture. Interactivity today are video games with sometimes very questionable content.

In contrast, the Internet is dominated by over information and the Medusa syndrome. That is why the creation of new value systems and quality concepts is a priority. Free uncensored thinking must make new post-democratic systems and forms of society possible—away from retrograde thought structures, fake news, nationalism and conspiracy theories. New media practices should be an aid to this, not the content. And if the Internet should collapse, we must return to analogous ways of transmitting information like carrier pigeons.

Question 3

Christoph Ernst & Jens Schröter: It would be interesting to know for younger readers socialized in contemporary media culture, to whom today's "media convergence" seems normal (which it is of course not, historically speaking), in what way the distinction between "television" vs. "computer" represented a contraposition at the time. At later stages of digitalization, it was often pretended that everything "digital" had nothing to do with television—that is, television quasi being an "old" medium. *Piazza virtuale* shows very beautifully, in our opinion, how distorted this contemporary view is. But what was the situation then? Did you see "digital culture" as something that was perceived separately and independently from an "old" media culture of television? Or more simply: What was your view of computer culture in contrast to the established media?

Karel Dudesek: Thanks to the numerous pirate radio and television projects, we were able to gain very good experience of how the media, radio, television and the computer were embedded in society. Television was established, regulated by law and, if necessary, protected by executive power. The computer culture was a new young, unregulated medium, growing and only operated by specialists. At the same time as the *Piazza virtuale* in Kassel, the *Mosaic*-browser was launched for the first time in California. Accordingly, the Internet was hidden in the background (underground) and television was in the foreground. We tried to combine these two media to take advantage of each other. The computer user was frightened back then and only felt safe in his own home, where he knew his way around. While the TV viewer was in a coma, condemned to silence. He could only cling to the remote control. The computer user had a mouse and a keyboard and maybe a microphone and could already communicate.

Benjamin Heidersberger: For decades, public television was the one-to-many "Leitmedium" of society. This claim was cemented in socio-political, as well as technical terms. The technical requirements for a signal with broadcast quality were virtually impossible to meet by amateurs. Then, in 1984, former state broadcasting was liberalized, and with it came greater diversity of opinion and access to the advertising market. On top of this came public access broadcasting, which enabled every citizen to become a broadcaster himself (*Kabelpilotprojekt*, Ludwigshafen 1984).

Parallel to this transition, the shift from analogue to digital took place and a powerful network, mainly broadband Internet today, was set up which could transmit these signals from many-to-many. With the invention of the personal computer, compression and digitalization of media, devices were developed with which the borders between amateur and professional equipment disappeared.

Our projects often display this hybrid working method between "amateur and professional", as well as "analog and digital". *Piazza virtuale*, for example, piggybacks on existing analogue TV and telephone

	as a return channel, but also uses computers and modems, while *Service area a.i.* is already partly taking place in a digital virtual world. It was during this time of upheaval that *Van Gogh TV's* experiments took place, which, as a political dimension, simultaneously represented conquest, emergence and empowerment.
Salvatore Vanasco:	We experienced computer culture in our youth, demo disks with gametrailers, WLAN parties, alternating hackers, artists who aimed for collective perceptions and processing, interdisciplinary cultural projects, which were precursors of design thinking and art thinking. Filmmakers who wanted to offer several narrative strands that were prevented by media carriers and media transports. Actually, it was a stagger between aspirations and the lack of tools for them, as well as, and above all, the lack of technical networking between citizens. At that time, we also investigated and dealt with *BTX*, *Apple Online*, *Compuserve*, *The Well*, *Minitel* and *Italtel*. We were constantly investigating their potential and did not yet find them at a technical level and a level of social outreach comparable to the "Leitmedium" television. We also made several trips to pilot projects on interactive television in the USA, in order to directly engage with the aims, the incentives and the promises of these corporate projects. Everywhere we saw that more and more computers and networks that used different bandwidths of transmission developed usage concepts that were the forerunners of the smart home, smart cities and smart citizens. It became clear to me that computer networks, multimedia,

	telematic applications and communication through computers, that is, digital development and digital networking, would make a new society possible. For me, I understood that it was a wager with time as to which applications could become mass applications through computers and networks.
Mike Hentz:	In the sense of polymediality, computers and television were equal tools for us. In the art scene in general, however, computers were classified as culturally inferior and not necessarily worthy of support. In this respect our unbiased approach was innovative. With the help of computers, we tried to bring television back to its original interactive level. In this context, it must be remembered that these attempts took place before the introduction of the Internet, i.e. computers were not yet interactive in the form in which they are used today. Still, with their help we were able to create programs for the interactive usability of the medium television. The connection of computers, telephone and television with the help of interfaces that we constructed made the interactivity of our television broadcasts possible. This was an enormous technical and financial effort under the conditions of the time. For example, I installed the entry points for the approximately 30 piazzetas worldwide, i.e. I have personally been to Riga, Paris, Zurich, Moscow, Prague, Berlin, etc.
	To the so-called "Hochkultur" our project was inferior or was ignored. The artistic context was not recognized. That made us combative. We had to defend our project permanently. *Piazza virtuale* was mainly

perceived as a platform of representation and not as an artistically interactive experiment. Many could not understand why we were invited to the *documenta* with an "inferior" art project.

The then Belgian director of *documenta*, Jan Hoet, had invited us not only for artistic motives, but also for *documenta* political calculation. He wanted to break up the self-righteous established circle of self-appointed German video curators, who until then had decided what was interactive video art—and thus worthy of promotion and exhibition—and what was not. Jan Hoet approached us as representatives of the next generation of media and video artists. The invitation to *documenta* was a "knighting" and recognition by the "Hochkultur" for us. The artistic dimension of our project with the media television, telephone and computer was only recognized years later.

A main criticism of computer art at that time was its "artificiality" and "technicity". The complicated technical handling of the computer, but also the artificiality of the artistic end product, e.g. electronic music by the band Kraftwerk, were recognized as art or an artistic process, not as "Hochkultur". The "technoid" stood in contrast to the higher valued "naturalness", the authentic, human expression in painting and music.

Even today, the handling of computers in a performative context is still difficult to use tactilely. The faders, buttons etc. are very small and restrict human motor skills like a corset. The technical difficulty of the computer to serve as an interface between

a natural, pleasant movement and function of the body and an artistic product is complex and has to be programmed very elaborately.
But electronic music can return this lost connection to the human body. Michel Waisvisz has tried, with the development of his synthesizer stick for dancers and body, to make an extended motor function possible when using music computers. The Theremin or the Chaospad can also be interpreted as such attempts.
A further problem in our work was that in the early 1990s, the content of television programs had to be considered "valuable" and "Hochkultur". These relative values were checked by many editorial meetings before a format or contribution could be broadcast. Live television was considered an incalculable risk. Especially our broadcasting format, in which EVERYBODY could participate unchecked, was of course predestined to be abused as a platform by nutters, nazis and other idiots. We (and especially our censor Katrin Brinkmann) were very much aware that the content of the broadcasts could derail in unwanted directions. But we accepted this risk in favor of artistic freedom and were also able to convince the responsible persons of the broadcasters of our position in the end. The lack of orientation of the national television stations at that time ensured a vacuum for us, which allowed us to try out unconventional and new things on behalf of artistic freedom. Even our sponsor and station negotiations and the political and dramaturgical mediation work were part of

our artistic project as an "Expanded Performance": the various "roles" were assumed by a well-rehearsed "Impro Team". All of this was inseparably part of the *Piazza virtuale* project. Our independence in this "game" towards the station managers of 3sat, ZDF etc. resulted not least from the experience we gained in 1988/1989 as illegal pirate TV with *Van Gogh TV*: we were technically able to realize and broadcast our project "illicitly", independent of public funds. Our goal was always to broadcast—a failure of our project was out of the question for us.

Question 4

Christoph Ernst & Jens Schröter: After all, "imagining" or "envisioning" a new medium does not only mean abstractly making a change for the future, because the "new" is always a promise for the future. Rather, our imagination as a "power of imagination" always comes into play when we think about possibilities. We would like to take a closer look at this thinking about possibilities. Because due to various factors, e.g. the expertise that someone has in a particular field, not everyone imagines the same thing. This inevitably creates a problem: different ideas of what is considered technically "possible" in the first place must be coordinated and regarded as "desirable" (and thus normatively binding) by all participants—especially in a project that is not based on coercion but on idealism. How did this "committing" or "swearing

	in" to the technical possibilities of the pursued basic idea (i.e. interactive television) work in concrete terms in *Piazza virtuale*? How did reflecting on the project's possibilities work during the earlier stages? And almost more importantly: the project was an experiment. Experiments have a creative momentum of their own, regarding unexpected (and therefore deemed impossible) discoveries. How did you handle and mediated such surprises?
Karel Dudesek:	The basic idea of *Piazza virtuale* was mainly conceived by Benjamin Heidersberger. I think it was immediately clear to all of us that this was the right way, no ifs and buts. Perhaps it was in fact the case that only Benjamin understood the *Piazza virtuale* to its fullest extent. After all, he ultimately had to guarantee the technical implementation as well, being the only one who could think and implement this technically. I for my part simply trusted him completely. However, I think that in the beginning we all didn't know where the path would take us and only the trust among us made it possible to realize the impossible. This is a—I would say—superhuman configuration that can only work rarely and for a limited period of time. Intuitively, without contracts among ourselves, we trusted each other and the cause. In post-rationalization, I understand why this could not continue to exist, because a few months later, more or less the same people who had previously held together were falling out with each other.
Benjamin Heidersberger:	From a technical perspective, the basic idea was to use the Touch-Tone system

on the audience side to control processes in the studio, in addition to the return channel with voice *via* telephone and data *via* modem, which we had tested in other projects. Thereby two out of four distinguishable tones were mapped on the 4 × 4 matrix of the telephone keypad, providing the viewer with 16 keys. The system had been a basis of the worldwide telephone network at the time since the early 1960s and was used for the well-known telephone hacks by Captain Crunch (early 1970s), who also came into contact with the later Apple founders Steven Wozniak and Steve Jobs during this time.

At the beginning of 1991 I had the idea for a prototypical tic-tac-toe, which was programmed on an Amiga by Rainer Koloc using a decoder chip. The Amiga could already generate a TV-compatible video signal then. Later a multi-channel telephone interface was built with our self-developed circuit board. The protocol programmed by Christian Wolff was based on this interface, which later on controlled the studio and the different broadcasting formats that Ole Lütjens realized with *MacroMind Director* as well. Thus, the development followed along a technology and not a philosophy. Obviously, the idea was expandable enough that we were able to implement more and more new ideas before and during the course of the project, so to speak as an operation on the open heart. The input often came from the team or from observing user experience.

Of course, not everything always worked immediately, but that is perfectly in line with today's practice in the computer industry, where unfinished products are delivered without operating instructions and are first fixed in practical user operation. Our way of working was equivalent to that of a modern start-up. Due to the obviously experimental character of the project and the close cooperation of artists, programmers and technicians, we were able to react to problems immediately, often while the show was already in progress. Generating a TV image ("broadcast quality signal") and controlling the studio by computer was by no means state-of-the-art. The 3sat/ZDF technicians in their governmental thinking certainly had to have some tolerance when there was no signal for minutes, the color vector was not locked or the boot screen of a Mac was visible.

As I recall, decisions were made as a team on the basis of individual competence, which could even mean that someone was able to realize their specific idea of a broadcast format.

Salvatore Vanasco: The new medium was already there. Interactive applications such as *Macromedia Director* or *Hypercard* were already in our environment, communities such as *The Well* or *Habitat* by Lucas Arts had already been realized, and so we already had an instrumental basis here. Storytellers, designers and picture designers, sound artists, composers and musicians were already active prior to that. We brought in the hardware technicians, the network technicians and the software developers, and we already had an extended interdisciplinary approach. The languages and the designations were different in each discipline, and one of the most important goals was to condense what was different into one language realm without losing what was special in each. What united us, however, was the possibility and the will to change something. The more technologically skilled then derived technical requirements from the joint discussions, and designers the design possibilities. However, the performance of the computers used and the transmission speed of the networks of the time set limits to the design possibilities. This was also included in the set of instruments. We had already learned the basic understanding for the development of the approaches at *Hotel Pompino* in 1990 and put them into practice together.

Mike Hentz: To put it very briefly: the "gang of four" consisting of Karel, Salvatore, Benjamin and me was the core of the project. We were the ones pulling the strings, we were the ones responsible and we finally made the necessary decisions.

From *Minus Delta T* of Karel Dudesek and me, *Van Gogh TV* developed, which was joined first by Benjamin Heidersberger and later by Salvatore Vanasco. We had previously worked together in other constellations and groups. For example, at Benjamin and Karel's Low Band Society, which was actually a video studio: there we edited our 1989/1990 *Van Gogh TV* projects. In 1990 we managed to rent the craftsmen's house Koppel 66 in Hamburg, where we set up and expanded our lab. Through the private equipment of Benji, our *Minus Delta T*-equipment and others a pool of equipment and possibilities developed. Since we were very well connected, friends, filmmakers, artists, and other interested parties such as hackers from the *Chaos Computer Club* Hamburg and Amsterdam quickly joined us. Students from the *Hamburger Schule für Bildende Kunst*, where I started teaching in 1989, also wanted to join us. Away from the established art business, we created a place of innovation and creativity with our lab. We offered a wide range of technical equipment of the newest generation, a lot of space and a group of intelligent creative people from various disciplines and fields of work, who were eager to explore new, unknown fields of work and tasks. Everyone was open and could try out. Everybody could also develop their own projects—as long as their main focus was on our projects. Sometimes we also managed to pay small salaries of about 500DM per month for the members of the team. Though, the motivation of the contributors was not money, but the unique free and creative working atmosphere: there was a shared spirit to work on something really new and important. Everybody learned from everybody, everybody could contribute their ideas and was taken seriously. Everybody was proud to be involved with individual projects on their own responsibility and had the feeling of belonging to a kind of "elite" or "avant-garde"—even if this was not immediately obvious to outsiders ...

Karel, Salve, Benji and I together acted as mediators, canvassers, team leaders, and idea generators. We prepared the *Piazza virtuale* project for almost a year. We set goals and pursued ideas together with the team, the implementation of which was monitored, supplemented and developed in weekly meetings. In the event of financial bottlenecks or deadline pressure, we as a "gang of four" set the priorities in a thoroughly authoritarian manner. The team accepted our authority, but always smiled upon our stress. They could always concentrate on their projects in the lab, while we, busy with acquisition and negotiations, were permanently on the road.

In terms of work, we were always aware that plan A (everything works and the financing is in place) was almost never possible. With Plan B only half of the realization or financing worked and with Plan C there was actually no possibility at all. We lived with constant cutbacks, but also with positive surprises, for example when a sponsor unexpectedly stepped in or new opportunities arose.

In addition to the endless ideas we had and which developed, we were enriched by the experience we gained and the ever-growing know-how we acquired, which constantly opened up new possibilities. In permanent brainstorming, a cross-fertilization took place, which generated countless new ideas.

The main question for all ideas was the possibility of realization. I still remember our approach very clearly: Benji or somebody else started to cook and we kept thinking and researching. This way, piece by piece solutions—maybe not always perfect prototypes—came out. In any case, the end result was always a clear analysis of the time and material expenditure and thus the feasibility.

This process was exciting and thrilling for everyone involved. In this way, our lab also developed step by step. Possibilities and solutions were constantly explored, with short-term or foreseeable implementations being regarded as essential. For example, a satellite uplink had to be discarded as too expensive. With the use of Panasonic picture phones we found a cost-effective alternative.

The team's commitment to the feasibility of the project prevented excessive dreaming and phantasms. The team spirit was a joint creation of a new and important project. Everyone tried to give everything, to do the best. In the independent work, a form of competition was also created, which spurred everyone on to further top performances. Thus, a sworn community with a gang or clan feeling developed. Own projects were put on hold and all energy was put into the common idea of *Piazza virtuale*. Outsiders were faced with a mystery and were astonished by the things we made possible. This generated not only admiration, but also envy and jealousy.

Question 5

Christoph Ernst & Jens Schröter: The previous question about the group's "uniting" *leitmotif* and ideas about possibilities leads to one of the most fascinating aspects of *Piazza virtuale*—the transgression beyond the boundaries of certain discourses or contexts of application. After all, *Piazza virtuale* was not only classified by you at the time as "media art". In the contexts in which the project is still remembered today, this categorization is still relevant. Yet it seems to us that the project was much more than "media art". It was actually an experiment on what was then a new form of realization of television, and consequently a new media practice. If we think a little further ahead, we reach the intersection between performance art and media use ("Use"), i.e. the dimension of utilizing the then new medium. *Piazza virtuale* can therefore be seen as a huge, and particularly globally oriented, social experiment on the use of new media, which equally makes the question of 'aesthetics' a complex matter. How would you categorize your project ex post? Perhaps in analogy or critical demarcation to similar attempts established in the early 1990s as well, to "methodologically" contain creative media design processes and make them marketable, such as "Design Thinking" (from 1991), which goes back to Terry Winograd, among others.

Karel Dudesek: Within the whole project in Kassel a team working simultaneously would certainly be an enrichment, as we did for example with the method—"Design Thinking", if it were adapted to the artistic concept. Figuratively speaking, it is not easy to couple the wagon of rational overkill of engineers and scientists to a running train like this project. But I think it would certainly have been interesting if psychiatrists, sociologists, hardware and software developers and many other professional groups and activists had actively participated in the *Piazza virtuale*. Actually, the leitmotif and the thought matrix came from performance art. Within *Minus Delta T*, Mike Hentz and Karel Dudesek had had years of experience in the field of music and performance art, and these motives for thinking and acting naturally flowed into the whole *Piazza virtuale* project, not only during the *Piazza virtuale* broadcast in Kassel, but also during the whole preparation period. It was a huge experimental set-up, not driven by commercial goals, but by artistic curiosity and wondering how far the train could still go. The project took place in a historical period, the dawn of technology, our ideas created demand even faster than it could be met by the industry, which breathlessly complied with our requirements and was happy that someone was actually using the latest equipment in real life. From cable-based telecommunications lines across borders, right through to satellite broadcasting, where anyone could freely receive our programming far beyond Europe.

Benjamin Heidersberger: The question of whether this was art or not did not bother me much at the time. In addition, we deliberately worked as a collective and in collaboration with the viewer, whereas the authorship demanded by traditional art is confusingly complex. Obviously, *the* art (Jan Hoet, the *documenta*, television, sponsors, viewers, politicians, the media) and the ideas of art gave us the freedom to carry out a unique and large-scale technical, political and social experiment. The project had its own pull on all participants, the spectators had their fun, art or not. I would have said at the time that we simply picked up and developed trends of the time and sleepwalked through connecting a few devices together. In the intermediate world of art and technology I see parallels to the work of my father, the photographer Heinrich Heidersberger (1906–2006). Photography began as a handicraft, indeed as an application of technology, and has become art, at least in part. In the 1950s, my father created algorithmic works (the "rhythmograms" as he called them) in the application of physical laws, which look like computer graphics, but are now art.

On the other hand, *Piazza virtuale* can certainly be classified in terms of media art/net art, but also Dada, Fluxus, performance, happening. At the same time, it was also an exploration of the possible applications of new technology. The industry quickly recognized this at the time and provided us with hardware and software without end. New boxes arrived every day. *Piazza virtuale* drained us financially and in terms of personal effort. We then tried in vain to find a way to accommodate the broadcasting format in Germany and continue with it. Except for art contexts like Ars Electronica, that didn't work out. The most open was actually NHK in Japan, who were interested in the future of television. In Germany, Giga TV (1998) and 9live (2001) were launched, which made gaming and call-in profitable. In the USA Karel tried to turn Piazza into a startup with the *Cultural Olympiad* 1996 in Atlanta as a tailwind.

After *Van Gogh TV's* collaboration ended in 1996, we continued working in different directions. From 1999 on, I put the Internet at the service of art ("Kulturserver—The Online Community for Art and Culture"). There, ten years before Facebook, the entire infrastructure was realized with a homepage construction kit, mail, chat, news stream, event calendar and video streaming ("Broadcast Yourself").
And finally: almost 30 years after the last broadcast at *documenta IX*, two German universities are opening the tomb, above which's entrance "Hier ruht Medienkunst" [Here lies media art] is written. If something else would have been written there, it might have remained closed.

Salvatore Vanasco: Several of us have been working for years with multi-user spaces and the cultural techniques of interaction and performance. One of the first conversations between Mike Hentz, Karel Dudesek, Benjamin Heidersberger and myself was about the transformation of the performance's resonance space and the possible points of interaction discovered there. We talked about the translatability of this culturally explored practice in tele-communicative communities and its possible spaces for action. We had experienced the first game computers and consoles. We saw the phenomena of arcade games and their potential, we studied technical protocols and their early varieties such as multi-user dungeons. We looked for technical and design translations and tried our hand at it with a number of very different projects. The character of a social experiment was given from 1990 onwards, as we then saw ourselves as test designers and test subjects. We did this by asking ourselves, what position could I take as an artist (architect, engineer, musician, etc.) and what meaning could this have for the respective project work. I postponed the issue of aesthetics, since I located us in an experimental arrangement of art, technology and society and claimed that making it possible should not fail because of aesthetic discussions. It was not yet clear to me what insights could and should be gained into which position and attitude, i.e. which disposition to this could and should be taken.

Winograd with "Bringing Design to Software", user-centered thinking as a new paradigm in the development of software were phenomena of that time and demonstrated that culture could enrich and improve interaction with machines. This stemmed from the engagement among thought, design and technology in the intertwining of knowledge and the extraction of telematic landscapes to create new spaces and forms for social encounters and the negotiation of cultural mechanisms. Of course, we had many prejudices and fears about industrial developments and their economic potentials. As early influencers, we tried to inform people, politics and industry through our projects and the experiments that took place in them, and to point out the potential of these untapped new reservoirs of cultural spaces and technologies.

Mike Hentz: For Karel and me, the combination of Expanded Performance, live art, "Lebenskunst" and polymedia art has always been the focus of our work. In our previous projects of *Van Gogh TV* and in the artistic tradition of *Minus Delta T* we have always tried to explore these connections and their limits.

This exploration of extensions in the sense of the above-mentioned media as the (sensory) prostheses has always included social, political and philosophical contexts for us. We have never been exclusively interested in our art and the technical implementation associated with it. We found this scenic monoculture to be inadequate for fulfilling the context. Performance took place for us in ALL contexts—not only in a gallery or on a stage for an elitist (art) audience.

As early as 1982 in the Bangkok project we dealt with the topic of media mysticism. We understood this to mean the shift in values that occurs when the same content and the same form is presented in different contexts. For example, the same song is perceived differently depending on whether it is performed in a cathedral, on an opera stage, on a marketplace or even in another country. Depending on the environment, the same product is perceived as either high quality or banal. These connections were clear to us from the beginning of our work together. That's why we had very high demands on the best possible adequate form and quality to convey our content—without becoming commercial or trivial.

Of course, the implementation of this claim did not always work as we had imagined. There was a certain number of mistakes and also misunderstandings.

However, we never saw this as a mistake or failure, but as part of an ongoing learning process. It was always important to us to make this learning process transparent for everyone, the constant elimination of mistakes and thus improvement of the product was a common process of the collective. This kind of work and art process was in line with our idea of a transparent public laboratory or studio. We had developed this way of working since the Bangkok project: the truck was studio, stage and living space. Later, in Europe, we implemented the concept similarly with the *Ponton*-bus.

This way of working and implementing art was in contrast to the production processes of art that had been prevalent until then: the conceptions and their implementation were kept secret and took place in closed studios. Copycats or copyright may have been a factor there. Only the finished product/work was presented and exhibited as an individual work with an individual signature.

However, in our opinion, we were geniuses as a group or collective—and not as individual artists. Our early opening to dialogue with each other and its development into a "Multilog" was an essential part of our artistic work. Process and concept were prioritized over the final product. Especially Karel and I, as experienced and trained performance artists, suffered from the reduced "hello form" of the participating spectators. But we were in the service of the concept and therefore held back.

As already indicated, we had hoped for more from audience participation. But also, the process that turned passive spectators into active protagonists was interesting for us. Observing how the participants handled the prostheses (platforms/programs) we offered and how they evolved was very exciting for us. Unfortunately, we were not able to use and implement all the platforms we had designed, because we had too much to do in this project. High quality platforms such as TheaterTV (an interactive role play on current topics) and the Interactive Monument (the development of a new democratic value system) were therefore not realizable.

With regard to Terry Winograd and his approach to design thinking, we saw media as prostheses and aids rather than independent content. We were primarily concerned with enabling human interaction—in a collective. For us, media such as video games as independent content represent systems that are separate from human beings. For us, the isolation of the individual in virtual worlds was more or less the same as escaping from reality through drug consumption.

Question 6

Christoph Ernst & Jens Schröter: A question about the infrastructural dimension of the project. You were sitting in your container at the *documenta*, having to keep the shop running. This, on the one hand, must have had a strong social component, i.e. responsibilities like some kind of personnel management, public relations, etc. On the other hand, there was this highly heterogeneous technical infrastructure, which not only had to be set up, but also maintained. Science and technology research use the term "infrastructuring" for this. Roughly speaking, the term refers to the work on often network-shaped and usually invisible, i.e. implicit, infrastructures, thanks to which we have clean tap water or a television picture on the screen. Can you outline from your respective perspectives how you have perceived this work in and on the infrastructural "backend"? For example, how did you deal with problems of different computer system standards (Atari, Commodore, Apple etc.)? What happened in case of crises and failures? Did viewer feedback translate into concrete technical changes? It would be particularly interesting to learn how the work on the infrastructure has also changed the idea of what *Piazza virtuale* in particular or a new interactive television in general could be.

Karel Dudesek: The inter-compatibility of the various technical standards, from hardware and software to the transmittable signal, had already been worked out previously in Hamburg at *Ponton* by Christian Wolf, Salvatore Vanasco and Benjamin Heidersberger. The local live production and coordination of a team of about 90 people was an enormous challenge. During the 100 days of broadcasting, new hardware and software modules were developed and tested. Regarding the programmatic aspect for example the implementation of censorship was an interesting step, how far can the process of censorship be delegated to the viewer. Another enormous field of work were the piazzettas, which were organized and supervised by Mike Hentz and Kathy Rea Hoffmann. In my opinion, the main didactic task was to convince the artists in the individual piazzettas that it was not necessarily just about self-presentation at the *documenta*, but also about further local networking within the respective cities in which the piazzettas took place. This was not always easy, since the medium of television simultaneously tempts one to exercise power, where suddenly individuals who have the sovereignty over an infrastructure also believe that they have the right to decide on the aesthetic or content quality of others. Actually, this is diametrically opposed to the basic concept of the *Piazza virtuale*, which was intended to manage without the classic presenter, show master, editor or artistic director.

Benjamin Heidersberger: The conception and management, but also sponsoring and financing of *Piazza virtuale* was in the hands of Karel, Mike, Salvatore and me. First of all, because we worked together with a large team, where everyone was responsible and self-motivated to advance their ideas. The vision we created together guided us all. In addition, there was also a support team such as administration, breakfast, visitor support, etc. The same people who were in charge of a part of the development were also often part of the broadcasting team. We were broadcasting live on average 7 h a day (and at night) with about 25 people, which is quite a feat. We lived in Hannoversch-Münden in a shared house and made the drive every day. Despite a relatively precise planning of course a lot went wrong. People oversleep, people and machines break down, money is lacking. But as if by a miracle we always managed to broadcast.

Similarly, the shared vision linked the various computer systems together. The video signal was generated by Macs using the Panasonic video mixer WJ-MX12, the fax receiver was a NeXT with video output, the central broadcasting control was a PC. The ISDN videophones could output PAL composite video, the Panasonic videophones (Visual Telephone WG-R2) 60 Hz video in black and white, which in turn the Panasonic Mixer WJ-MX12 could read. The telephone interface processed analog plain old telephone system signal and output audio. All connected to the RS-232 interface of the control protocol.

In my notes from January 7, 1990 I find the sentence "Decode the Touch-Tone to Control a Brush". On April 3, 1991 there is the first sketch with tic-tac-toe over the telephone, which was the basic idea of *Piazza virtuale*. From there the system has developed further to a multimedia communication system on television.

Salvatore Vanasco: Through past joint projects, we knew that there were different areas of responsibility that needed to be determined and the respective newcomers trained. I saw these as areas of competence for which the one or other previous qualification was already in place and could be conveyed in conversation and in the laboratory practice of the *Ponton European Media Art Labs*. So, we virtuously mapped out crafts and their key areas of performance, learned how they operate and passed that knowledge on.

We knew television studios, we knew computer networks, we could broadcast television, we could develop and produce television formats, we were familiar with computers and their operating systems and the web as a platform for all operating systems was not yet in existence. We wrote network protocols to mediate between different network topologies, we soldered computer boards and wrote the software converters. We always helped ourselves and nothing seemed to be unsolvable.

We never perceived any problems, we were able to counter many things with intelligence, initiative and diligence. This spirit, which lay at the core of us all, drove us and brought us to solutions. We regarded each format as a further development from previous occupations. With most of the collaborators we had a long working history and so we were able to develop continuously together.

Hence, the project of an audio community from 1989 to 1991, *Hotel Pompino*, Ballroom TV, *Piazza virtuale* and the *Service area a.i.*, are a continuous and interdependent process with temporary fixations and formations. Every experience gained was incorporated, questioned, processed and related to each additional project. We knew that new phenomena are created through networking and we were constantly in pursuit of them. Furthermore, the question in which discipline the best applicable methods were available drove us forward as well. Since the broadcasting formats, and thus the realms of events, were constantly changing, these changes brought about other phenomena of possible circuitry of information, communication and interaction. Communication on a 2D surface has different desires than meeting in virtual three-dimensional space. So, we learned that what we took away with us from interaction and resonance points in performance, we had to concretize and offer in a different way in a two-dimensional image. Furthermore, in a three-dimensional, virtual event space, analogies of physical space very quickly reach the limits of cybernetic space constructs.

Mike Hentz: Working in the containers was already very special. On the one hand, the containers offered a private space, which was secured by door codes or keys and only accessible to us. This was absolutely necessary because the whole construction and technology was fragile, expensive and also very sensitive. In addition, we didn't want to take any risks and keep out uninvited curious people and unknown hackers. We were also concerned that our station might be stormed and taken over by others.

On the other hand, there was a public space directly in front of the containers with an entrance point, camera and monitor, so that the visitors could follow everything on the monitor. We also had a "Coffeehouse", where Wu Shan Zhuan not only served coffee, but also exhibited documentations and the concept of the project. In addition, I had created a design for the exterior of the containers, which also explained the function and concept of *Piazza virtuale*.

Reimagining *Piazza virtuale* 153

At the entrance in front of our container castle there was a separate storage container. On the first floor there was an office with a telephone and a conference room. In addition, there was the actual broadcasting studio, which was made up of two containers. In the lower containers were computer workstations and a separate recording studio. Nobody lived or slept in the containers. Nevertheless, the lab was in operation almost 24 h a day. This included many night shifts from us.

But we also had to deal with other problems of an infrastructural and individual nature: the team was housed in a house outside of Kassel, which was difficult to reach. In addition, we had an apartment in the center of Kassel at our disposal. It was located above the disco *New York*—these were all very spartan, dark sleeping quarters in which practically no social life took place.

Our social life took place almost exclusively in the container-city. When the weather was good, we sometimes celebrated parties outside the containers, but in the broadcasting center such parties were absolutely taboo. There were daily meetings for technical coordination and weekly general meetings. In addition, weekly meetings were held to determine who, when and what program was broadcast and which piazzettas were to be involved. The results were communicated and coordinated mainly by fax and telephone. It was technologically very complex and a great sense of achievement every time we managed to connect at the right time and see that everything went as planned.

For the technical feasibility it was essential that we had spent months beforehand transplanting the Hamburg *Ponton*-lab to Kassel. During this time, we worked intensively to ensure that the various computer systems and interfaces were compatible with each other. The satellite uplink technologies were also installed and were thus soon operable without special knowledge. The programs were newly developed and continuously improved. We were able to minimize the downtime due to computer crashes by using backup computers on which identical programs of the broadcasting computer were loaded.

In order to maintain the broadcasting structure, at least four to five people were always needed. Two operators handled the computer technology, a sound technician as well as a communication officer for the connection to the piazzettas and a program officer. The program officer prevented the misuse of the platform, e.g. for National Socialist content). In addition, someone from our "gang of four" was always on site. These were usually Karel, Salvatore or Benji as supervisors in charge or as "firemen". Since I supervised the piazzettas directly on site, I was present less often. This task was also quite exhausting and time-consuming: the technical conditions had to be checked and compatibility had to be ensured. Especially abroad, with the different systems at that time, there were always new challenges. Actually, this was supposed to be done outside airtime, but the tasks were so extensive that this was almost never possible. So, it happened that even during the broadcasts many things were running in parallel.

All in all, it can be said that this was a frontier experience: we went completely up to and beyond our limits in terms of our work and social life. Outwardly, we seemed relaxed, but among ourselves, our nerves were often on edge. We called each other names in order to persevere. Like marathon runners we tried to motivate ourselves by pushing each other. The occasional visits to Heike Mühlhaus' designer bar *Das europäische Haus* and our two big piazza-parties, were no substitute for an actual social life. After the three months of *Piazza virtuale*, everyone had a lot to mend and repair. Friendships were destroyed, privately one avoided each other and tried to more or less hang on. The funny creative collaboration was at an end. It was frustrating and absolutely no pleasure to work on the project anymore because of the workload. But the common goal to create *Piazza virtuale* was the one that kept us going.

About six months after the completion of our project, we heard about a company in Silicon Valley that was working with similar systems. A well-paid team of 200 people had realized about 10 percent of what we had accomplished with a basic staff of 35 people.

In the end, we are immensely proud of what we have achieved. But we were completely burnt out. None of our "gang of four" was willing to repeat a project under these conditions.

My suggestion to go to the USA together, to analyze our project in a residency and then to restart it positively was rejected by Karel, Salvatore and Benji. After these borderline experiences it was no wonder that in the end individual and commercial priorities divided the group.

Question 7

Christoph Ernst & Jens Schröter: Tying in with the question of infrastructure: From the very beginning of our involvement with your work we found the conceptual step from *Piazza virtuale* to *Service area a.i.* very interesting and as well media-historically significant. On the one hand, the idea of virtual reality is clearly even more central to *Service area a.i.* On the other hand, the character of the interaction—and consequently also the dimension of use—of *Piazza virtuale* has been changed. Can you briefly outline how this conceptual change came about, e.g. to what extent it was intended as a genuine new development or rather as an improved (?) version of 1992 *Piazza virtuale*? What were the guiding ideas for this follow-up project and how does *Service area a.i.* present itself retrospectively, from your perspective?

Karel Dudesek: The *Service area a.i.* 1994 project, which Salvatore Vanasco was in charge of, was *Piazza virtuale's* move to include more spectators as participants, as co-artists. While *Piazza virtuale* allowed 4 or 8 spectators to become participants, *Service area a.i.* had 64 telephone lines and 64 computer accesses. Spectators, participants, and fellow artists no longer manifested themselves only on the television screen, but moved in a virtual world, which now offered a series of thematic "piazzas" at the same time, on which, similar to the program blocks of the Piazza virtuale, participants could paint, make music or chat together. The computers of the *Service area a.i.* were located in Hannover. This virtual world was expanded *via* the early Internet to Linz, Ars Electronica, where it was connected to "reality" with a stage. An SGI graphic computer projected the virtual world into the stage, a grid of speakers projected the sound of the world onto the stage and a tracking system enabled the rear projection of an artist from the stage into the virtual world. The television image on 3Sat was a studio production of this stage, which was oriented towards the artist on stage, i.e. it transmitted their impressions—image and audio—to the television viewers.

A dispute 1994 among the owners of Ponton later led to a split. One group continuing to work under the name Van Gogh TV moved to a small town on the borders of Hamburg, to work on the project "Worlds Within" for the "Cultural Olympiad" during the Atlanta 1996 Olympics. Axel Roselius, Ernst Pfannenschmid, Martin Schmitz, Karel Dudesek, Tim Becker and Manuel Tessloff, joined by Andreas Uthoff. The other part Benjamin Heidersberger, Salvatore Vanasco, Christian Wolf, Ole Lütjens and others remained in Hannover running Ponton.

Two years later (1996), the Van Gogh TV team (Martin Schmitz, Ernst Pfanneschmidt, Axel Roselius, Tim Becker, Karel Dudesek, Andreas Uthof and Manuel Tessloff) moved to USA, Atlanta,

New York and San Francisco. We went one step further with the project *Worlds Within* for the Olympic Games in Atlanta. In *Worlds Within*, hundreds of participants were now able to use their computers *via* the Internet to enter a virtual world and set themselves up there, "staking out their claim", i.e. setting up their own Piazzetta and painting or making music there alone or together with others, and using the results and artefacts to design their Piazzetta and make it into an event. Both projects were designed to allow participants to take part with standard equipment, *Service area a.i.* worked with a DOS PC, *Worlds Within* with a Windows PC.

Our servers where hosted at Wired in San Francisco for free. Louis Rosetto the publisher of the Wired Magazine was an early supporter and fan of the project. In a subsequent stage of expansion, in collaboration with AT&T and Bell Labs, an early audio and video bridge (like Skype later in 2003) was develop by engineers from the Bell Lab in cooperation with Ernst Pfannenschmid and Martin Schmidt. The plan was to set up a decentralized, distributed multimedia server system that was spreading across the whole of USA, in order to enable thousands of users to participate simultaneously with text, image, video and audio in a 3-dimensional world.

We moved to New York where Julian Simon and Michael Dodt joined the team. NBC provided for free a demo suit at 7 floor of the Rockefeller center, frequent evaluation meetings took place downtown Manhattan in AT&Ts studios in the famous Western Union building.

The million dollar fairy tale took an abrupt turn when the US government decided to antitrust AT&T and decided to divestiture the mothership in multiple smaller companies. Our partners disappeared and the whole project came to an abrupt hold. We moved back to good old Germany. More or less after 3 years, 1999 I decided to shut down the Van Gogh TV operation. Even today I think this US engagement was an invaluable learning process for all of us, but the difference in the team spirit to the early Van Gogh TV projects was that the projects 2.0 where overshadowed by the dot com ideology, which then later bursted in 2000.

In 2000 I was appointed to lead the media department at the University of Applied Arts in Vienna which was dreaming in an ancient romantic stage of "the early digital". Together with Martin Schmitz we upgraded the department towards a contemporary and modern environment for experiments for internet, digital tv, sound studio and divers labs with a huge financial injection from the former minister Elisabeth Gehrer.

As the greed from other departments of the Institute kicked in and the fear of Peter Weibel to lose his political control, I left Vienna for London. Their leading two master Programs at the Ravensbourne University, together with Michael Breidenbrücker. Soon our programs became one of the best interactive digital courses in the United Kingdom. There we introduced a cooperative discursive education model, which I also practiced in Vienna, where the students became mature partners, I at

	least in my function opposing classical teaching, but rather engage in a mutual relationship with the students. The benefit of the departments in London where that both pathways existed simultaneously, the artistic and the commercial format, each customized according to the students preferences. In London I had the joy to discover beside the Anglo Saxonian way of life, again my roots to Asia (1974 as student of Arnold Keyserling and later with minus Delta t "the stone project"). We had students from Taiwan, Korea, Japan, China, Philippines, Malaysia, Hong Kong and Thailand, with many of them I am still in contact. This lead after living and working eight years in London to my decision to move fare East from Europe, to a place where I have no DNA or language relations in 2008 to Beijing for another eight years.
Benjamin Heidersberger:	The user interfaces of the *Ponton/Van Gogh TV*-projects have evolved with the number of dimensions in them. In *Republic TV* (1989), it was the one-dimensional text interface on television, but which could be played live by the viewer *via* modem. In *Hotel Pompino* (1990), a three-dimensional hotel with 40 rooms in 2 Amigas was built in such a way that candidates could move from room to room in the virtual studio and trigger functions in it with hotspots using the software Vidi-Mice or Mandala. In *Piazza virtuale* (1992), the user interface on TV consisted of a sophisticated two-dimensional window technology (including video) from the now defunct company Miro. The limited

	number of users on the screen then turned into the 3D communication space at *Service area a.i.* (1994), which allowed the selection of a focus by a virtual camera. This approach has been further extended in the virtual learning environment "Comenius" by tools and the time dimension by storability; television has been omitted. Finally, in the *Kulturserver* (2000) a two-dimensional standard surface was used, allowing 20,000 artists to be online and offline in the system at the time.
	Since 1994 at the latest, i.e. since the work on *Service area a.i.*, we were firmly convinced that three-dimensional user surfaces were the future, i.e. "Rooms" instead of "Windows". Although a text-based massively multiplayer online game (MMOG) is also immersive through the player's imagination, real immersion is only possible with 3D, which is most similar to being in the real world. Eyes and ears work in stereo, the movement in space is a natural experience in life. It can be assumed that thought structures and reality models in the brain are three-dimensional.
Salvatore Vanasco:	The *Service area a.i.* was a conceptual further development of *Piazza virtuale*. While the TV screen surface was transformed by the inversion of the sender-receiver relationship into a central place of action for the production of democratic consciousness, *Service area a.i.* was a new place, a second kind of nature to be explored. The analogy of the poet, who is the only one who knows the old world and the new world, who at the event horizon peers from the world of television ahead into the three-dimensional, unexplored world

	and reports back to both sides, represents the change of disposition in thinking and possible action.
Mike Hentz:	*Service area a.i.* is, in my opinion, a further development in the direction of social networks. These interactive live broadcasts *via* 3sat proved to be a kind of hybrid version of *Piazza virtuale*, Social Media and Virtual Gaming and thus formed one of the forerunners of Second World. I only contributed to this project conceptually and was not involved in the actual implementation.
	During this time, I was more involved with the "real" groups in terms of content and art. In particular I researched their location on the net and on television. The interplay between image, sound, visual backgrounds as well as traffic technology and their orientation on the net played an essential role.
	In this context I developed the first reality TV formats in the Baltic States, Poland and Russia in the late 90s. In analogy to previous works, the combination of television and the net was also in focus. In addition to the classic Big Brother frameworks, school TV, content talk shows with an ethical focus, interaction with the audience as well as group behavior and responsibility in candidate tasks were the main focus.
	However, the follow-up shows experienced a rapid commercialization by the television management. This also included the idea of targeting specific generations. However, this was contradicted by my experiment of having different generations work together within a show, so that an end was put

to this work. All in all, however, it was necessary for my development in order not to lose sight of the mainstream of trends and possibilities and not to lose sight of my actual method of approach.

Question 8

Christoph Ernst & Jens Schröter: In conclusion: Looking at today's media culture and especially at the so-called "social media" and their database-driven logic of exploitation of social relations, what can we learn from *Piazza virtuale* (1992) and *Service area a.i.* (1994) for today's media culture? Do these projects—strictly speaking from your perspective and later experience—still have a message that can be extracted, as if from a message in a bottle? What would this message be (if it existed)?

Karel Dudesek: We are those bottles, 2020 a virus sent us a message, nuclear bombs did not fall on our heads. An invisible "something" put a stop to all the meaningless activity. Whoever follows "un-social media news" and fake news attentively nowadays, analyzes the conveyed contents, will realize what kind of state of neglect we have gotten ourselves into. Un-social media news is mainly about profiling and the exploitation of user data, which are later returned as data kraken, in order to either better manipulate the users or to get a better grip on the commodity society. Fake news (television and newspapers) have mutated into a product, which in the information mania automatically and unreflectively pass on news to each other. Serious research is "not anymore economically feasible" and is outsourced to private activists such as *belincat* and various leaks. *Facebook* does not operate their social garbage disposal in the Sunny Side of California, but with underpaid Filipino online censors, who are retiring after a few months and need psychological support to possibly survive the western mental garbage in good health. Post-Traumatic-Stress-Disorder of the "unsocial media news". *Piazza virtuale* did not participate in either mechanism. The political world today is incapable of action, the industry is at a standstill and lying in wait. Both groups swim like predators through this journey through time and hope that the consumer will return to their laps in good humility. The media are overflowing with coverage and outdo each other with morbidity entertainment, only the crime scene is presently real and not fictional. What is now wonderfully reflected is the sickness of this society, which has been driven into this condition by politics and economics. The economy and the entertainment industry are collectively engaged in the destruction of both environment and mankind, and politicians are watching with sweat on their brow, silent and helpless. The media is going at full speed and has reached the zenith of its god-dawning reportage/destiny, it is not the few murders or small wars that garnish the bomb lines, it is the sheer mass marketing of dead material, quote: "Folgen für die Wirtschaft, nackte Zahlen, blanker Horror" ["Consequences for the economy, bare figures, sheer horror"]. The virus has removed the veil from all this turmoil, so that it is all bare and clearly exposed before us, the naked truth. We will see if someone will draw some consequences from this. Artificial intelligence will not be able to put the veil back on, at least not for those who are not yet brainwashed. Of course, hatred and fear are inarticulate and widespread, and they fester in the sweat between widened eyes, in the resigned bodies of consumers. Because if they rise up and take to the streets, citizens are rewarded with tear gas and pepper spray. The citizen pays for his own legally regulated self-delusion, with his own tax money and radio license fees, just as he pays for the weapons with which the police or military, as for example in Hong Kong, will shoot at him in the end. *Piazza virtuale* would be just the right thing these days, because the interesting media life takes place in the fake news, leading article's commentaries and live streams on the internet, though these are unfortunately only text-based. In contrast, "Social Media News" can also post videos, but these are still not interactive. *Piazza virtuale* would be multimedia, interactive, live and orchestral, not a monolith where the creators hide in the *Piazza virtuale* but come and go in flux.

Benjamin Heidersberger:

"Social media" such as *Facebook* are presently based on the so-called "social graph", which depicts the interpersonal relationships as a data structure. This is a powerful tool that serves to monetize human traits, using addictive mechanisms to do so, with issues such as privacy and hate messages being insufficiently addressed. It is also unclear to what extent the algorithms used lead to the radicalization of users.

The projects of *Van Gogh TV* are, on the other hand, from a different time, connected to television as a "Leitmedium" that no longer exists today and are somehow more "innocent" because their mechanisms are more transparent.

With global pandemics like "Corona" we experience a strong push of society into the virtual, the missing human contact is replaced by telecommunication media and social media. I doubt, however, that we want to live in a virtual world like *Facebook* in the long run, where an absolutist ruler rules, where we have not made the rules, where an algorithm determines our circle of friends and our most human needs are monetized. And in the process subjecting ourselves to an alien value system. "Facebook friends" are not the same as "real" friends, sexuality and artistic freedom are nothing to be ashamed of. And we determine what happens to our data.

Should society, voluntarily or forced, increasingly live in a virtual world, we shall not want to give up democracy, separation of powers, laws, liberties and rights in the "New World", which we have fought for over centuries. Perhaps state action, possibly at a European level, is required here. However, I wonder as well whether we really want a state-run *Facebook*.

Salvatore Vanasco: An essential point, which concretizes the experiences we made and could make with our projects, was our illusion that we did not want to serve any higher authority (military-scientific complex, state, religion, economy as such) and refused to do so. This disposition is not inherent in the listed global takeovers. Every draft, every

	manifestation is subordinated to economic efficiency. We were cultural researchers of a culture that still had to settle and develop itself. We were still under the illusion of being free and autonomous to research and develop artistically.
Mike Hentz:	So, if I look at current media culture on the internet and media in general, I have to say that today's anonymity and localization on the internet up to fake news has not really provided any solutions. No real development has taken place, except in the areas of surveillance and security, where we are now looking at conditions as described by Orwell.
	Actually, a bridge between tactile reality and virtual appearance or resource should be built. But even in this area—probably due to a lack of commercial interest—there are still no satisfactory implementations.
	I had particularly high hopes for school television on the Internet. Although there was an educational follow-up project at *Ponton* in Hanover, there have not been any convincing implementations in terms of content either. There is hope, however, because although there is a lack of good projects in terms of content, great technical progress has been made. The Corona crisis in particular has quickly integrated the unloved stepchild Internet and digitalization in everyday school life into the social community.
	There are now countless chat rooms or communities that could be seen as successors to *Piazza virtuale*. Nevertheless, there is a decisive difference to *Piazza virtuale*: In these monocultures of today, there is no openness towards the "other". On the

contrary—virtual doormen decide who fits in. Other non-conformist opinions and dissenting comments are bullied, insulted, or subjected to a shitstorm. This inevitably restricts discussion and learning processes. I would like to explain what I mean by this by means of a concrete, exemplary piece of *Piazza virtuale*. In *Moby Dick*, an eleven-year-old talked on the phone with the captain of a research ship in the Arctic. The captain had prepared a scientific speech for television and was then effectively taken by surprise by the boy's questions, as the latter did not know what it was all about and had only landed in the program after an hour of trying to phone in. From this unexpected encounter a worthwhile dialogue developed. And both participants had learned that patience and openness can bridge gaps and enable virtual transfers between two very different dialogue partners.

In this sense, *Piazza virtuale* was extraordinary: people from different generations and cultures met and exchanges took place. Professionals had to become improvisation artists in a surprising context without losing face or content. These encounters were rare, but in the end these moments were what made us realize that we had not worked on this extraordinarily complex project for nothing.

For today's media culture, many research projects can be derived from the findings of *Piazza virtuale*. For example, the problems of location and identification in terms of content and responsible identification were already known from *Piazza virtuale*. Today, it would make sense to start a project on this topic with *Van Gogh TV*.

The twelve-hour John Cage Memorial Night, during which over 100 people performed without rehearsal or preparation, showed us how important timing is in such projects. There were many moments of glory that night, but to this day the question of timing is still central. Recording and processing information from ten people or more requires a multi-log with its own image and sound design and, so to speak, slower digestion. In our live set, a memory store would have been useful to be able to operate such functions as rewind, dubbing or even link restoration. Future projects with such or extended Multilog should be explored further, as this could lead to incredibly interesting symposia or other theme work.

Other ideas that were already being considered at the time, but have hardly been developed to date, would be interactive silent visual clapping, live emoji-commentary with people's location, avatars or identities. Now would be the time to get out of the development stage with that. Furthermore, content-based tourist guides through the dense caves of the Internet could be an interesting option. Considering the future of 5G, which allows real-time without delay, endless possibilities like live games and interactions, visual number databases as battles, dialogue up to multilogue as concerts, entertainment, games or learning processes could be realized.

When I extract a message in a bottle from all the experiences and reflections through *ct*, the first thing I would say is: continue, but become more content-oriented. Furthermore, I feel it is extremely important to work on collective qualities after all this time of individual and monoculture. These should not be affected by feigned rules of etiquette or politics but should enable us to have a real post-democracy in the global world!

The interview was conducted as an e-mail-interview with individual answers. After all answers were received, they were merged into one coherent text. The interview was originally in German and was translated by Leila Brehme. The editors would like to thank Leila Brehme for her great work and the members of Van Gogh-TV for providing such rich and detailed answers!

References

Heidersberger, Benjamin. 1991. Die digitale Droge. In *Cyberspace. Ausflüge in virtuelle Wirklichkeiten*, ed. Manfred Waffender, 52–65. Reinbek bei Hamburg: Rowohlt.
Heidersberger, Benjamin. 1992. Die virtuelle Piazza. In *Netzwerk-Dimensionen. Kulturelle Konfigurationen und Managementperspektiven*, ed. Johannes Ehrhardt, 124–143. Bergheim: DATACOM.

The manufacturer's authorised representative in the EU is Springer
Nature Customer Service Centre GmbH, Europaplatz 3, 69115 Heidelberg,
Germany. If you have any concerns regarding our products, please
contact ProductSafety@springernature.com

Printed and bound by CPI Group (UK) Ltd, Croydon, CR0 4YY
23/03/2026
02076745-0005